Tangled Up in Alaska

A Woodland Coloring Adventure

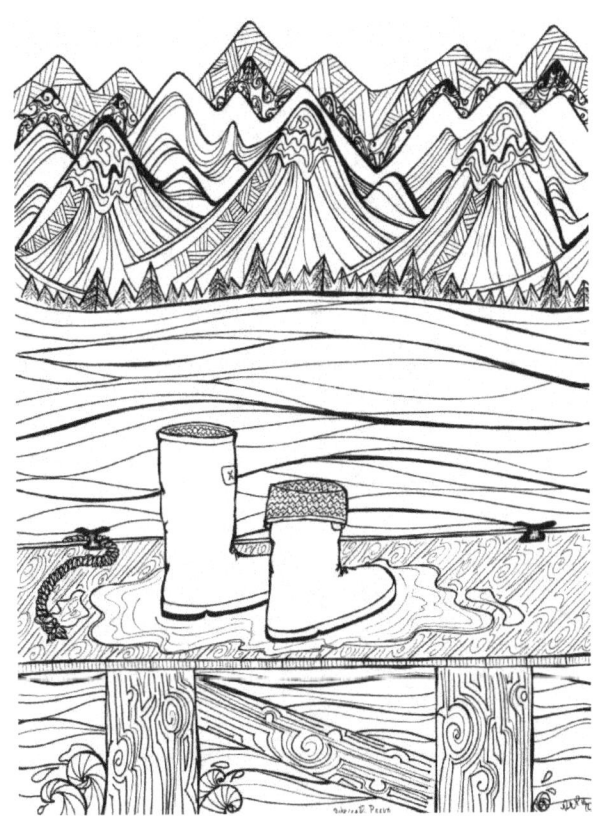

Hand drawn by:

Rebecca Paavo

Copyright © 2018 Rebecca Paavo

All rights reserved.

ISBN:198654267X
ISBN-13: 978-1986542678

To my loves:
BP, EP, HP, & little GP

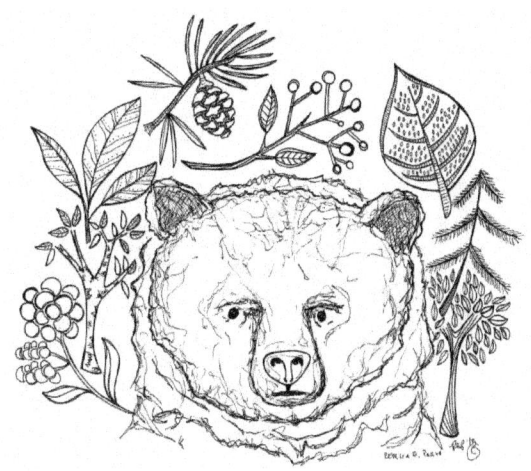

Soli Deo Gloria

Rebecca Paavo© www.sorrelwoodstudio.com

Colored with love by:

. . . .

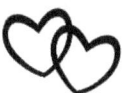

Come color your way through
America's Last Frontier

. . . .

And get zentangled up in

ALASKA

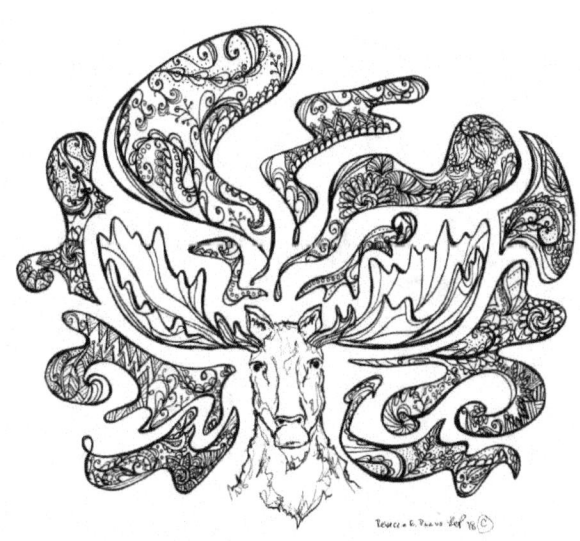

~Rebecca

Rebecca Paavo© www.sorrelwoodstudio.com

Rebecca Paavo© www.sorrelwoodstudio.com

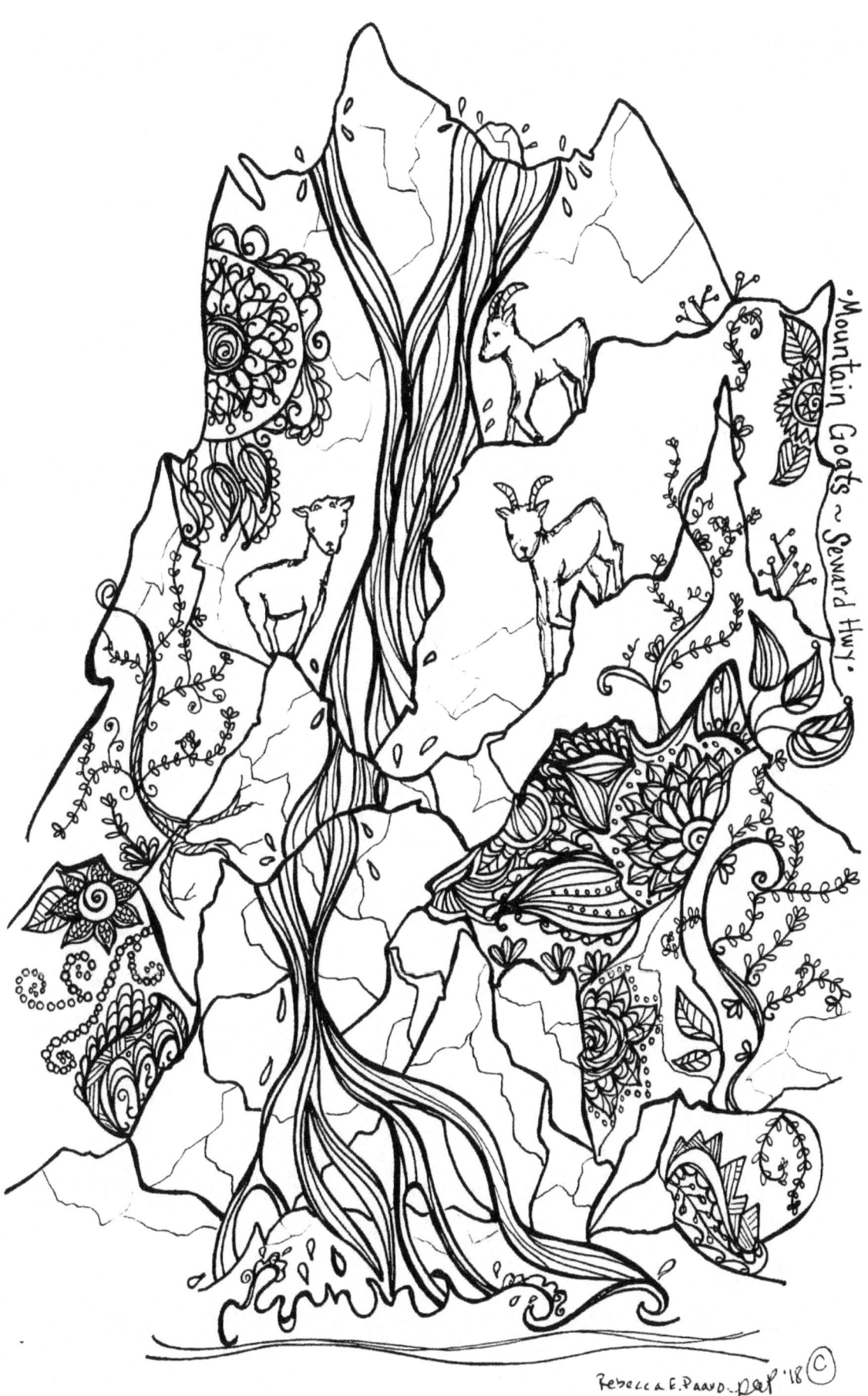

Rebecca Paavo© www.sorrelwoodstudio.com

Rebecca Paavo© www.sorrelwoodstudio.com

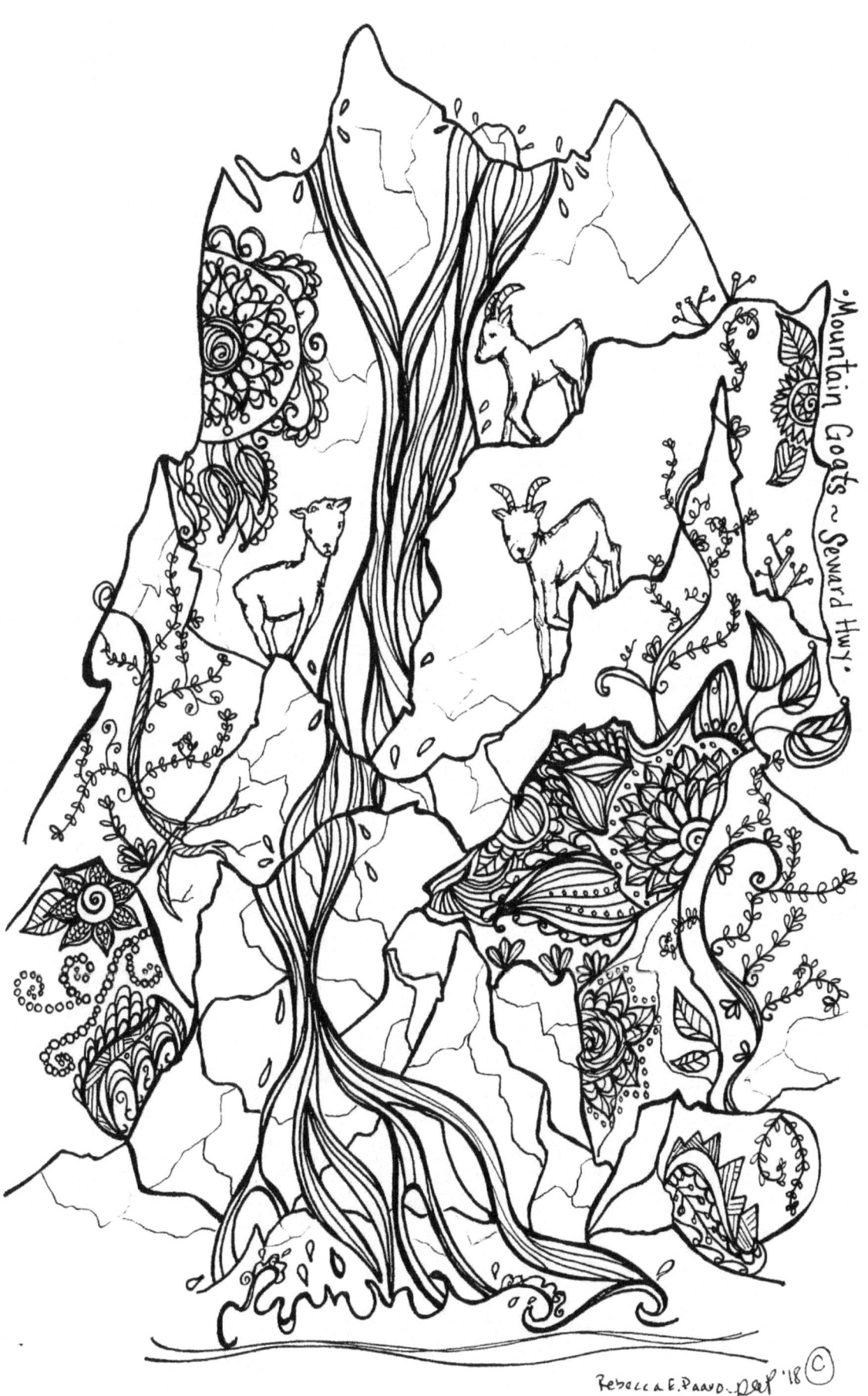

Rebecca Paavo© www.sorrelwoodstudio.com

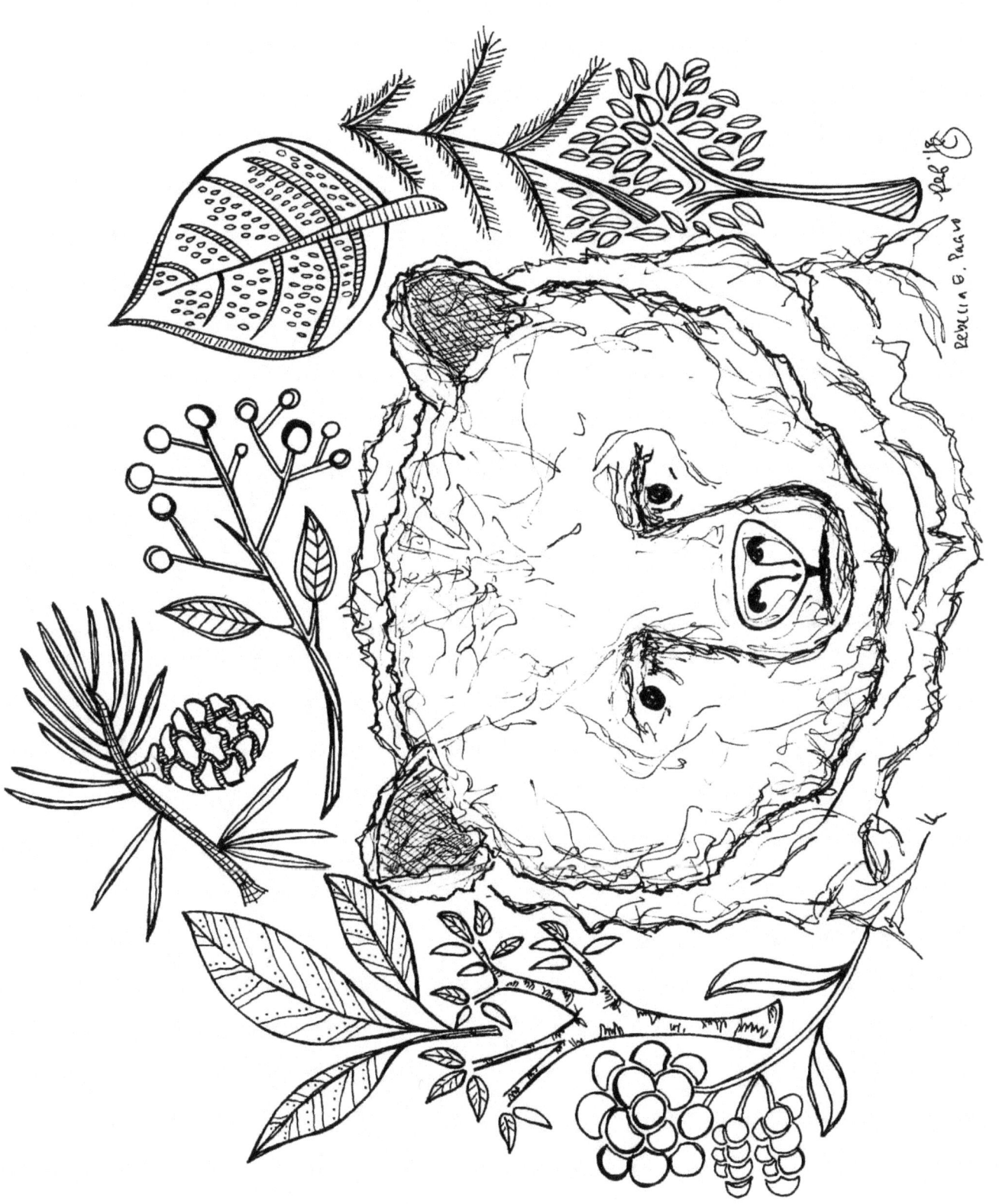

Rebecca Paavo© www.sorrelwoodstudio.com

Rebecca Paavo© www.sorrelwoodstudio.com

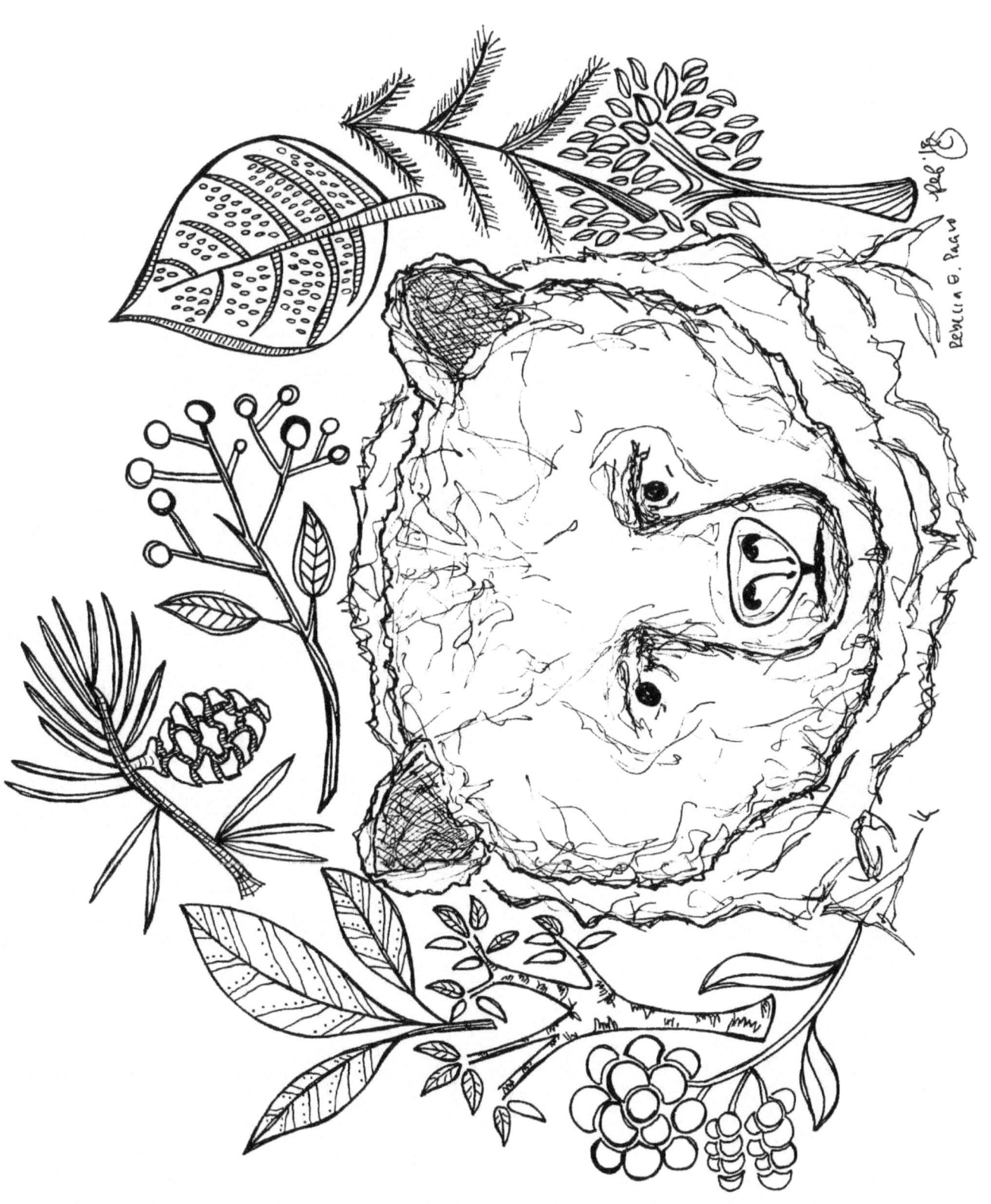

Rebecca Paavo© www.sorrelwoodstudio.com

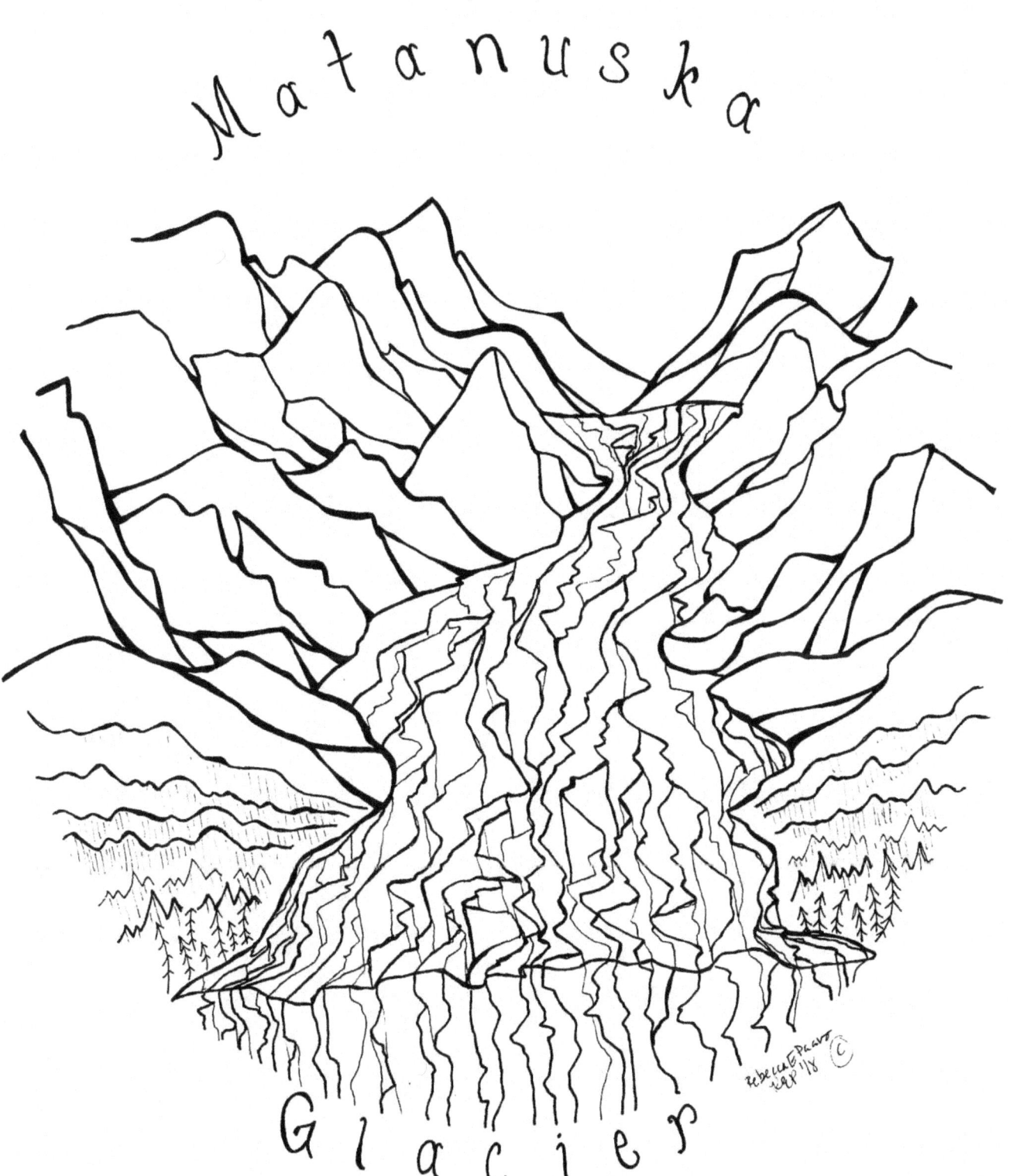

Rebecca Paavo© www.sorrelwoodstudio.com

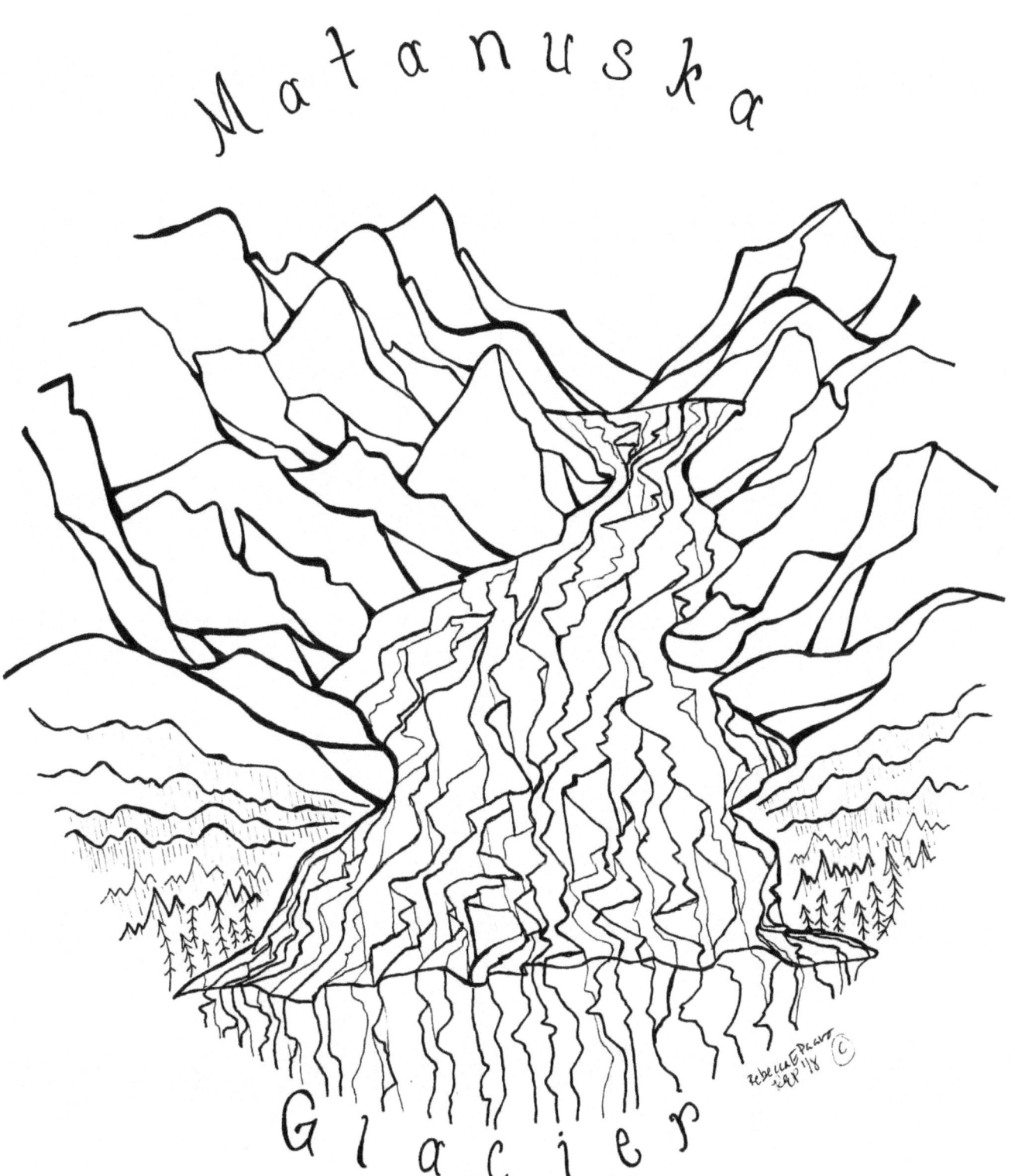

Rebecca Paavo© www.sorrelwoodstudio.com

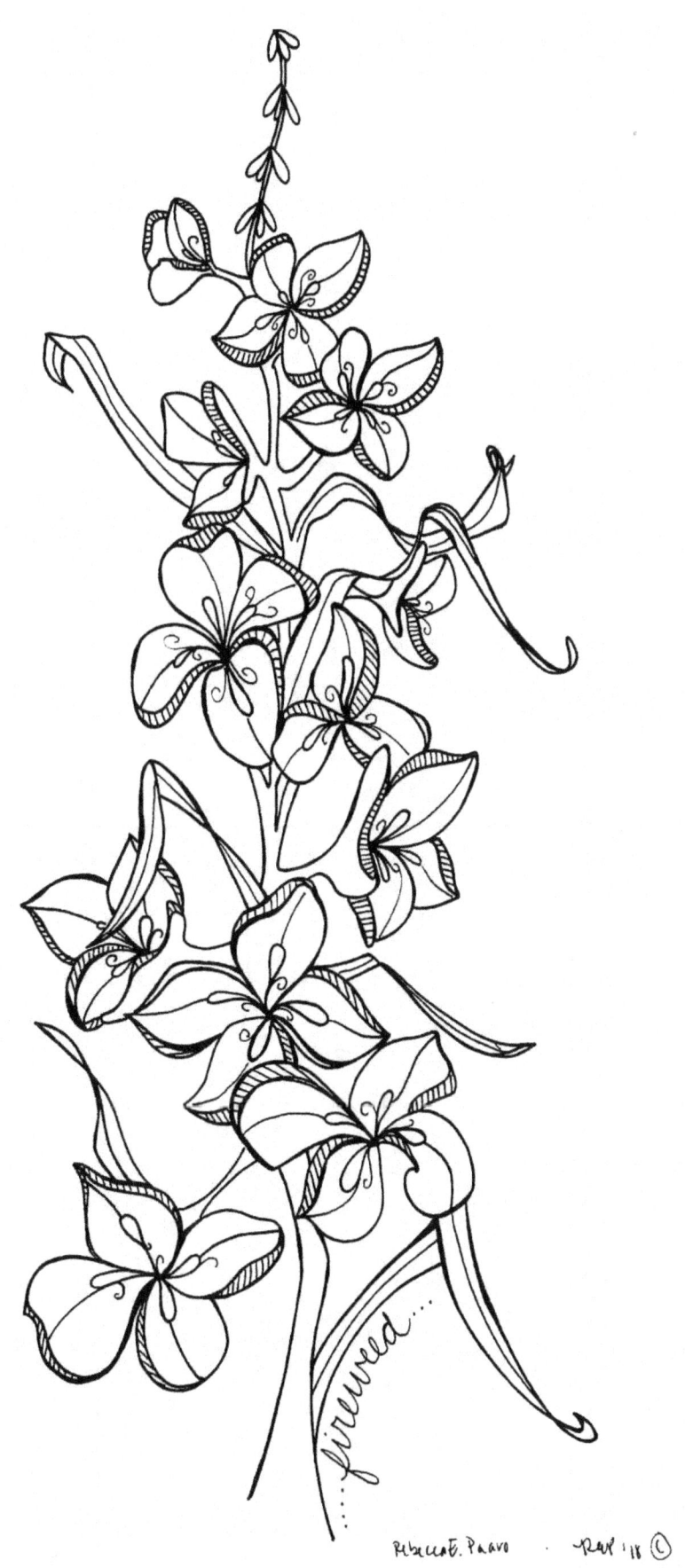

Rebecca Paavo© www.sorrelwoodstudio.com

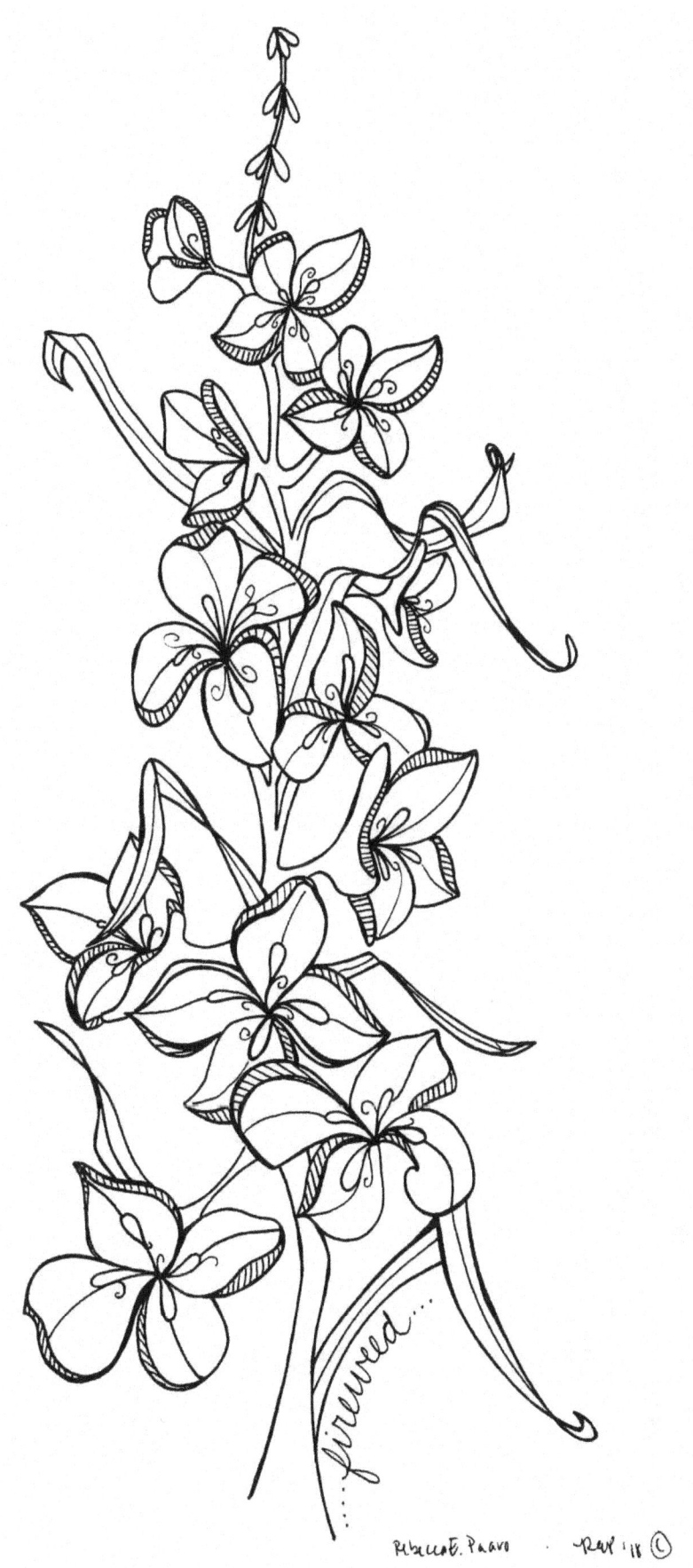

Rebecca Paavo© www.sorrelwoodstudio.com

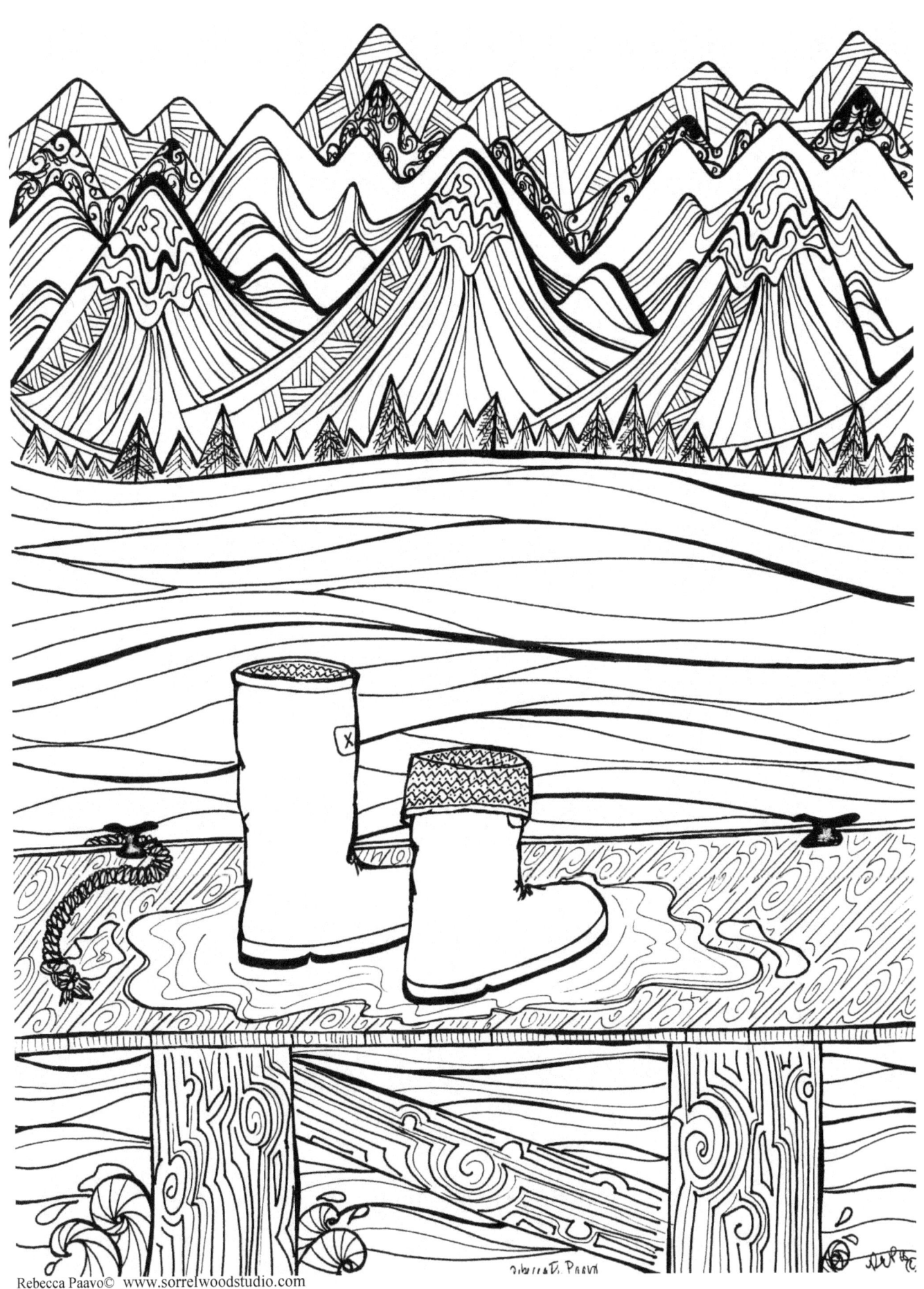

Rebecca Paavo© www.sorrelwoodstudio.com

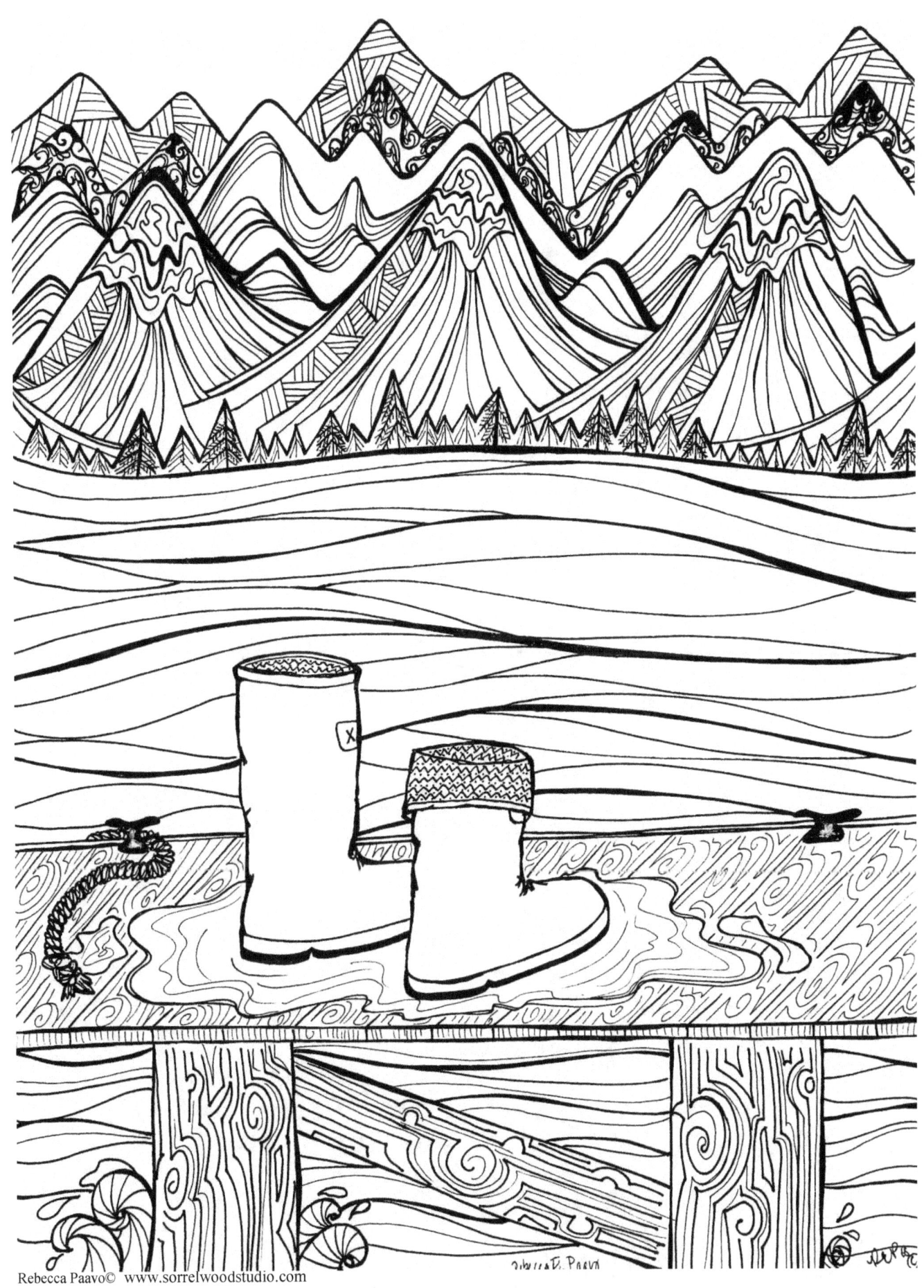

Rebecca Paavo© www.sorrelwoodstudio.com

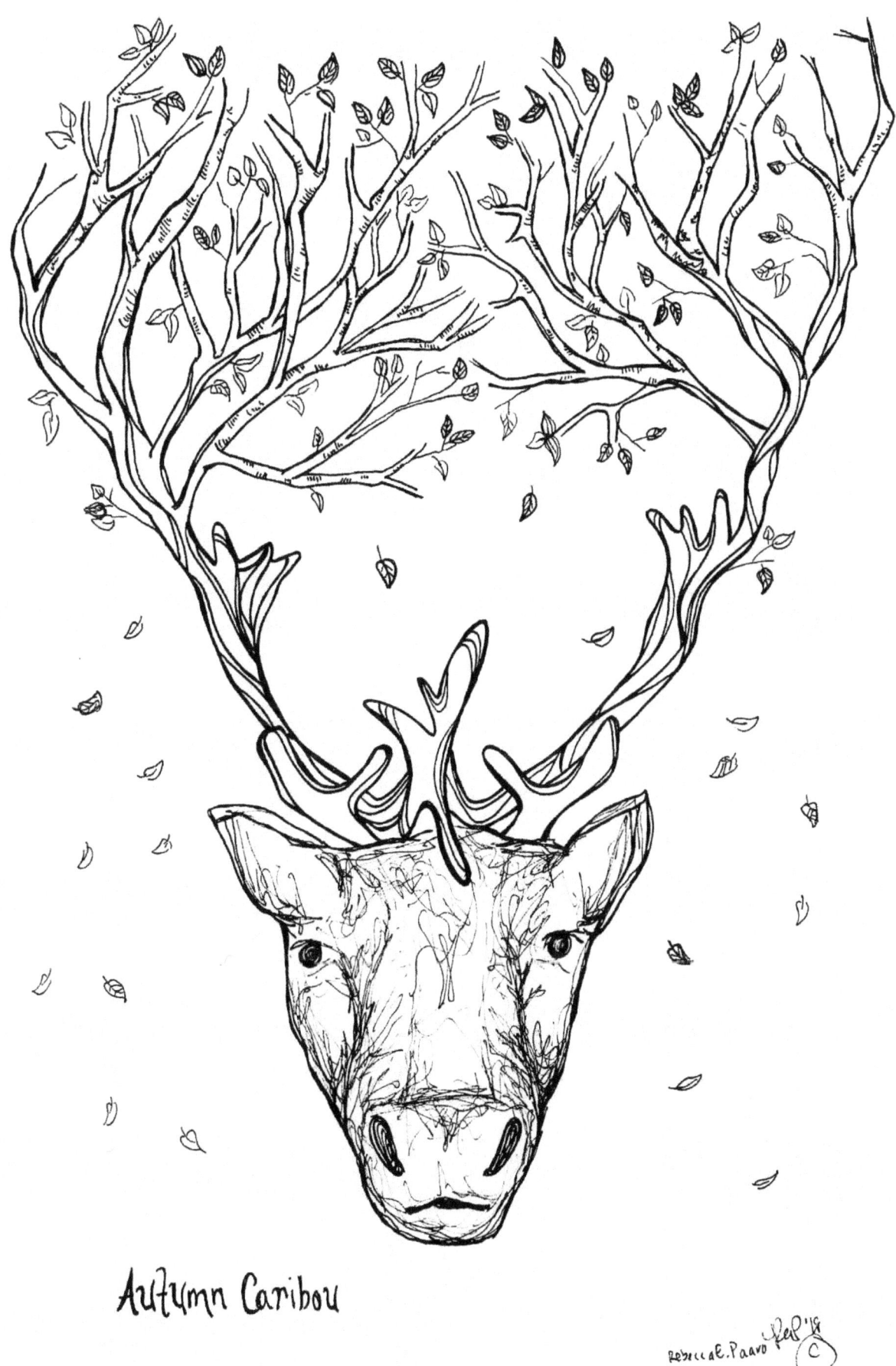

Rebecca Paavo© www.sorrelwoodstudio.com

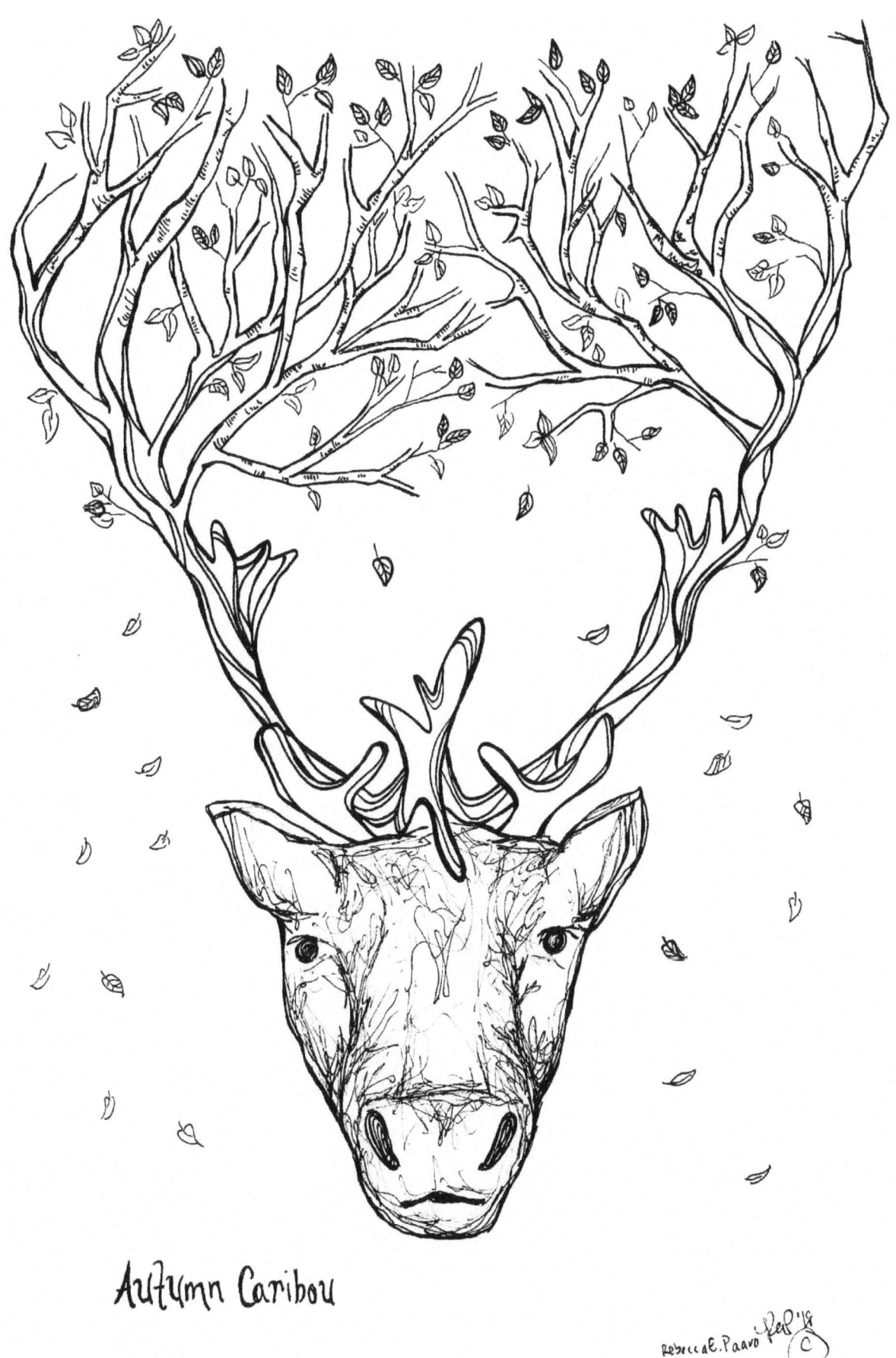

Rebecca Paavo© www.sorrelwoodstudio.com

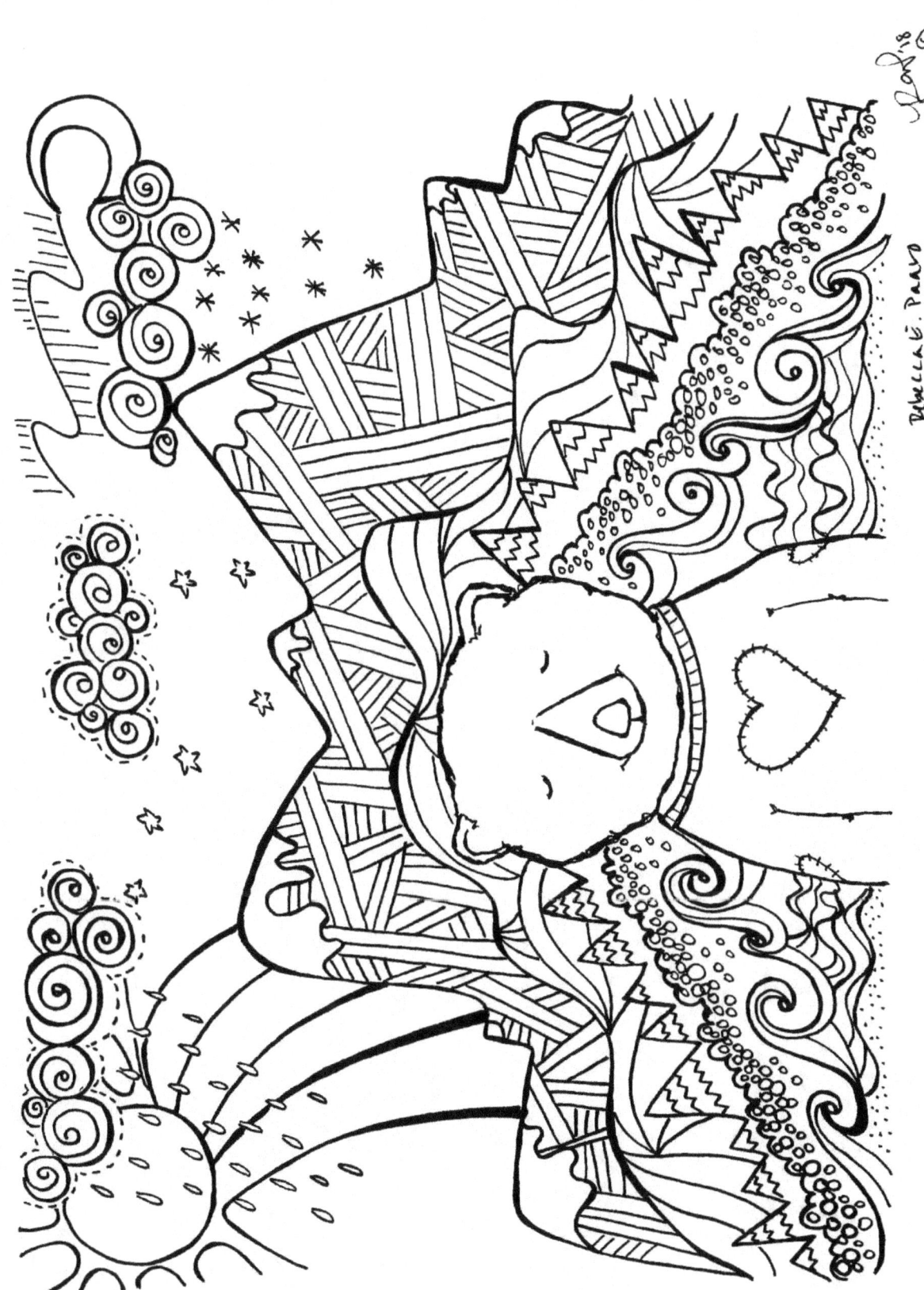

Rebecca Paavo© www.sorrelwoodstudio.com

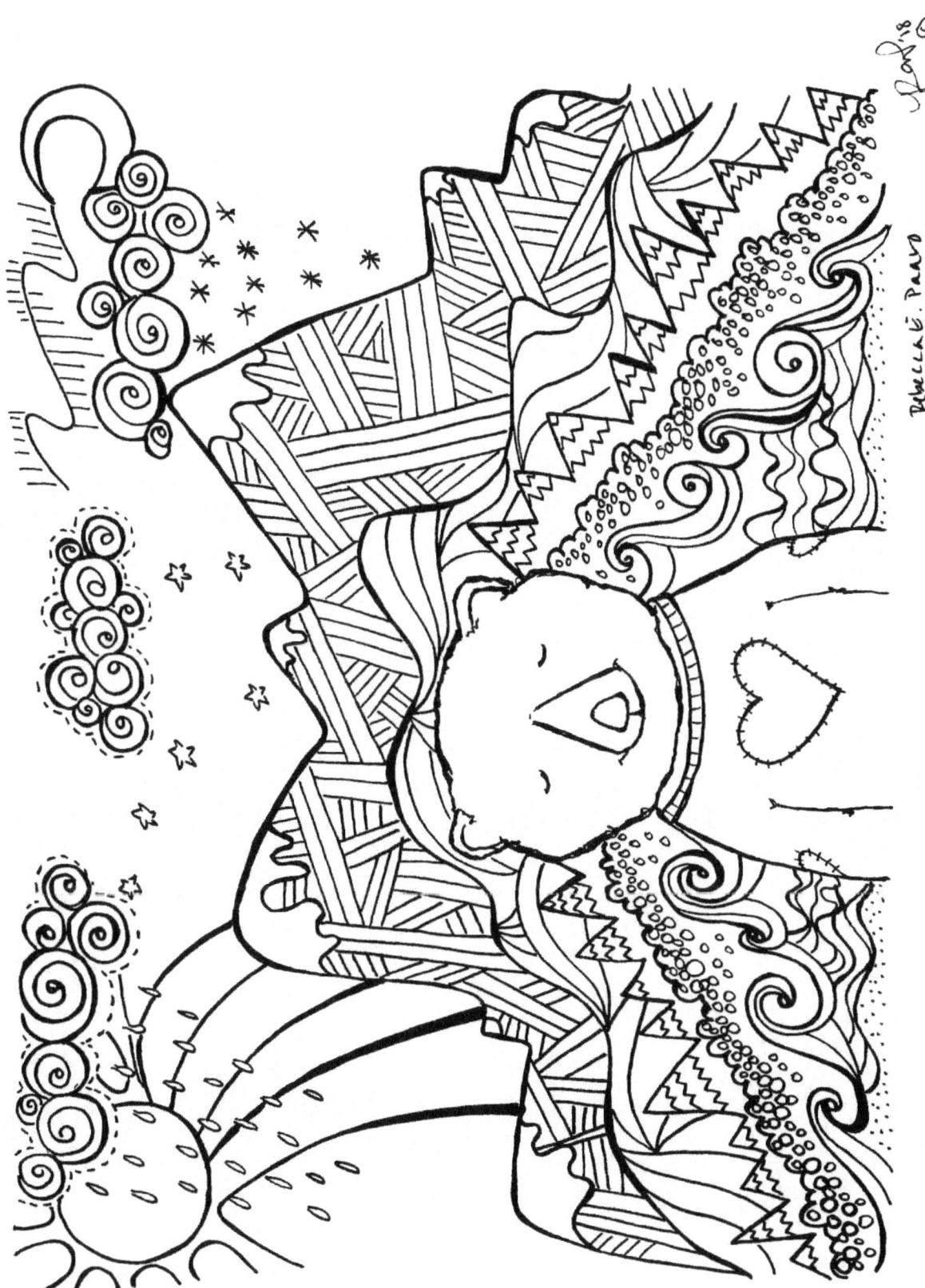

Rebecca Paavo© www.sorrelwoodstudio.com

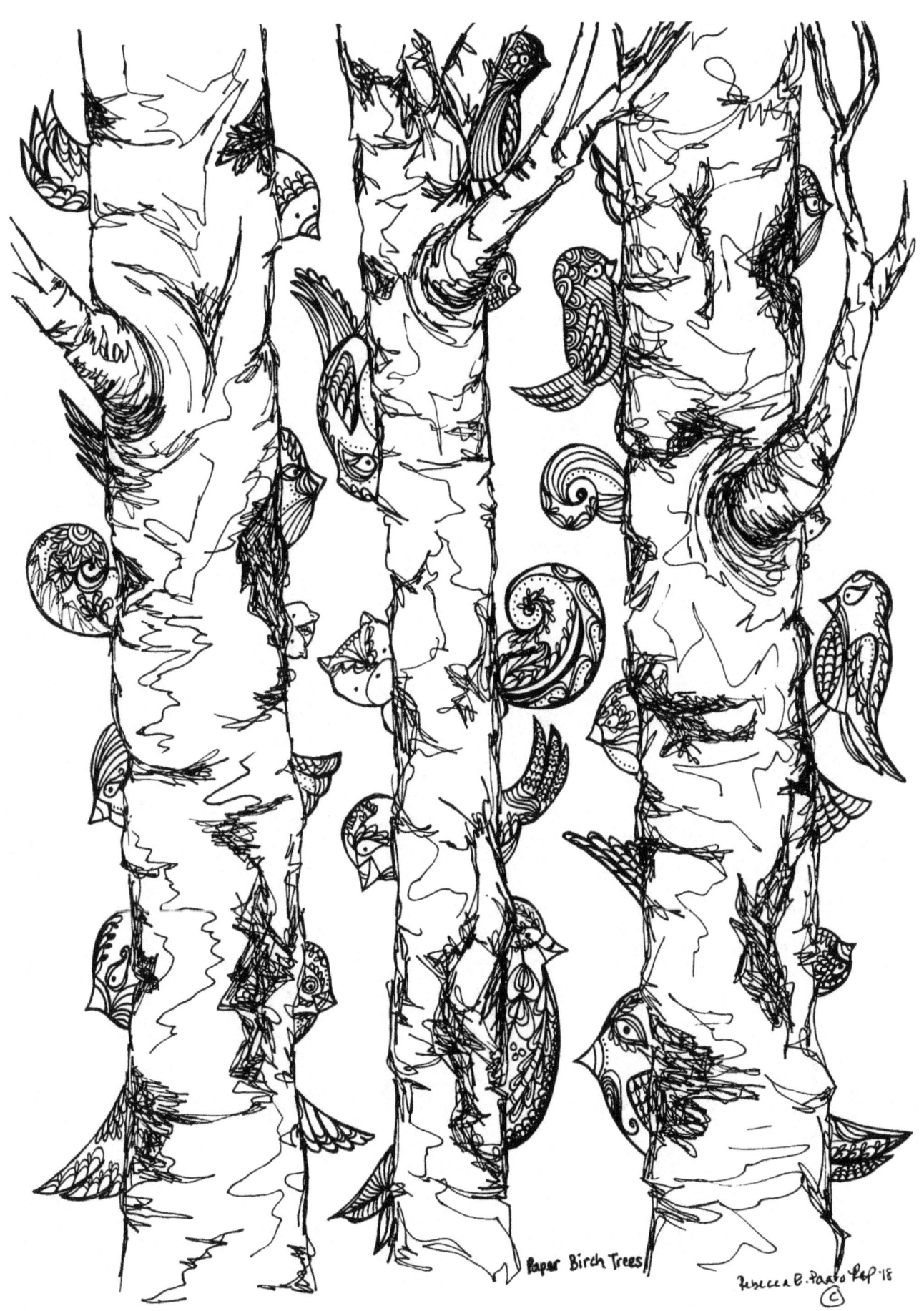

Rebecca Paavo© www.sorrelwoodstudio.com

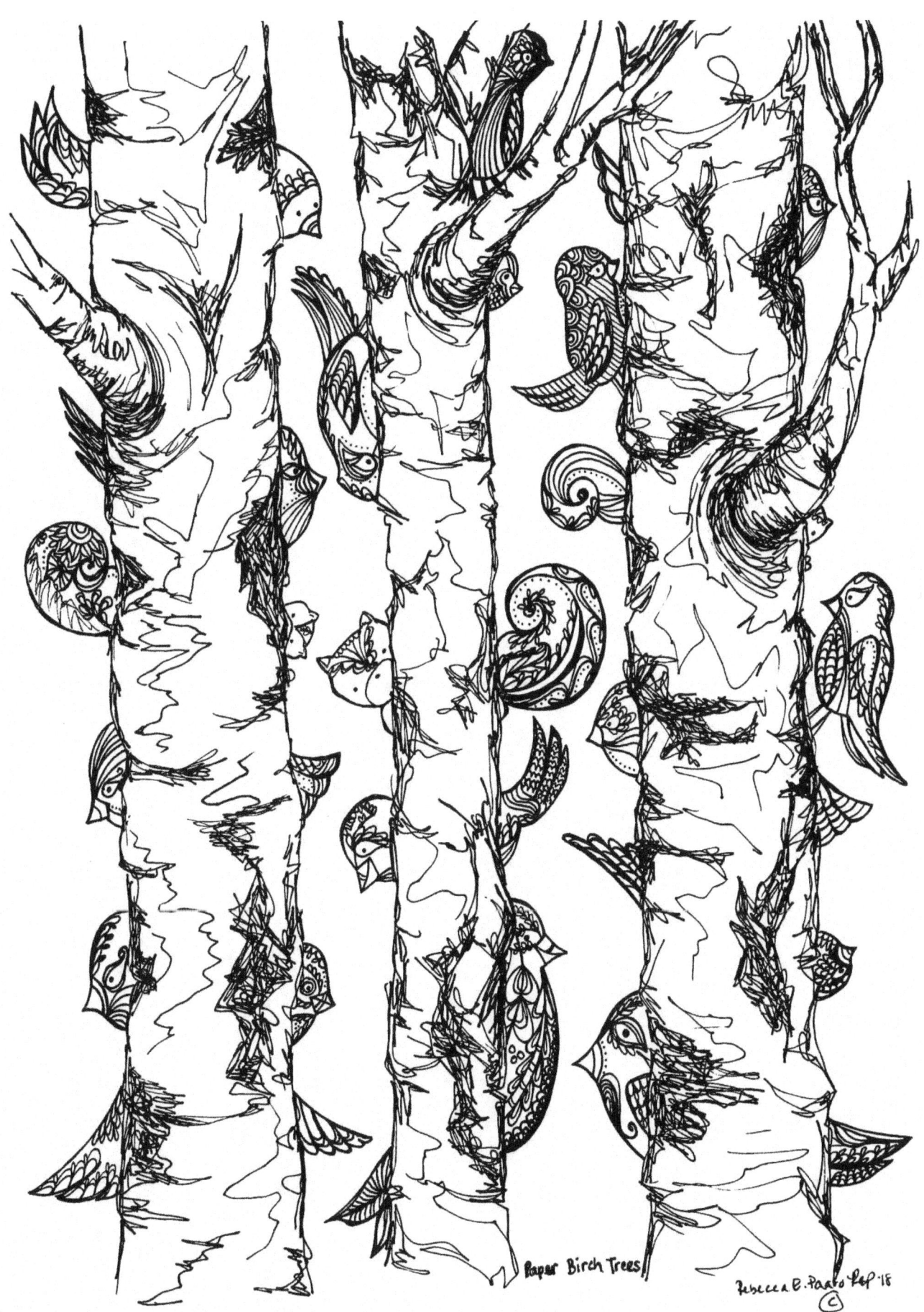

Rebecca Paavo© www.sorrelwoodstudio.com

Rebecca Paavo© www.sorrelwoodstudio.com

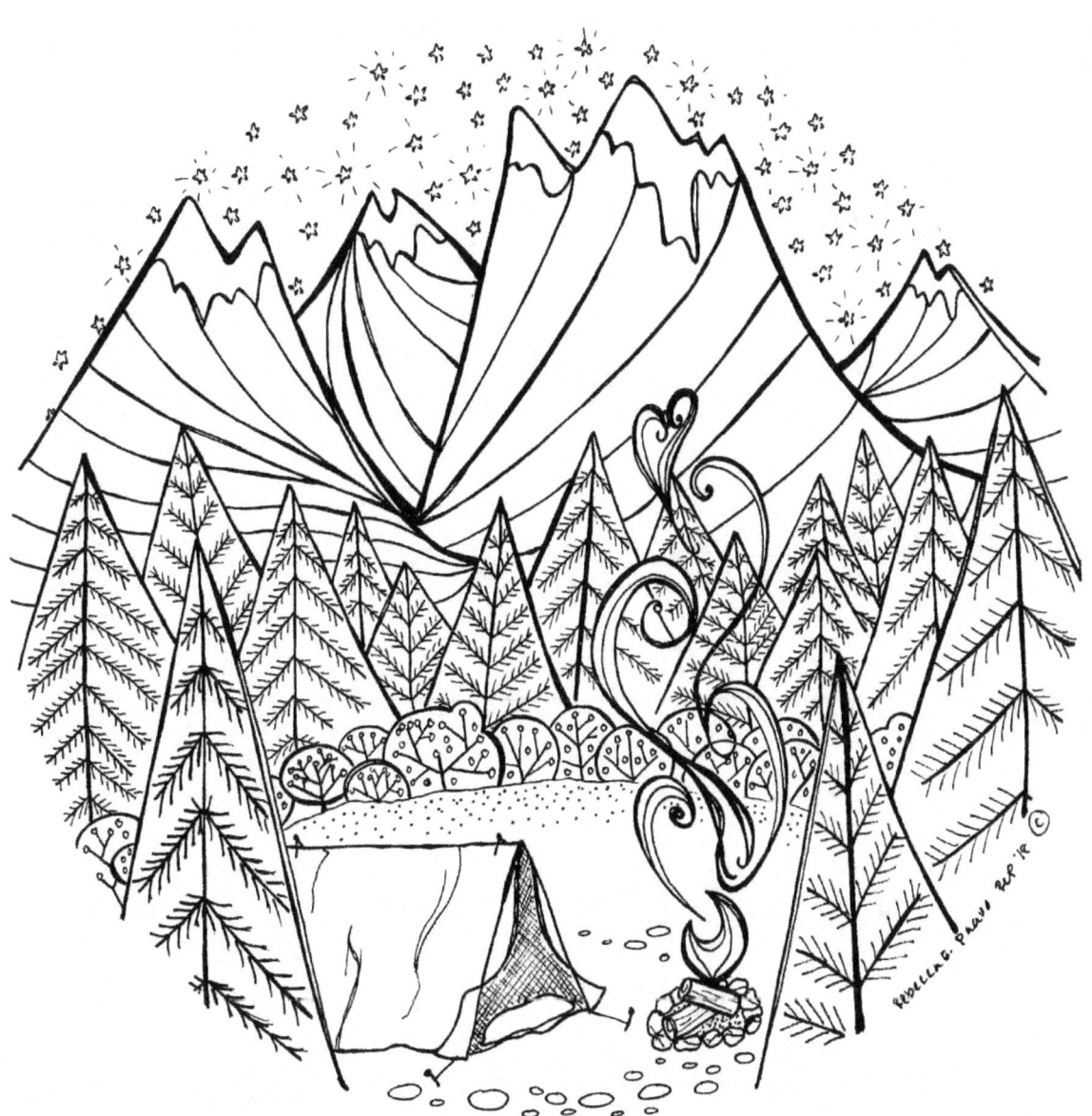

Rebecca Paavo© www.sorrelwoodstudio.com

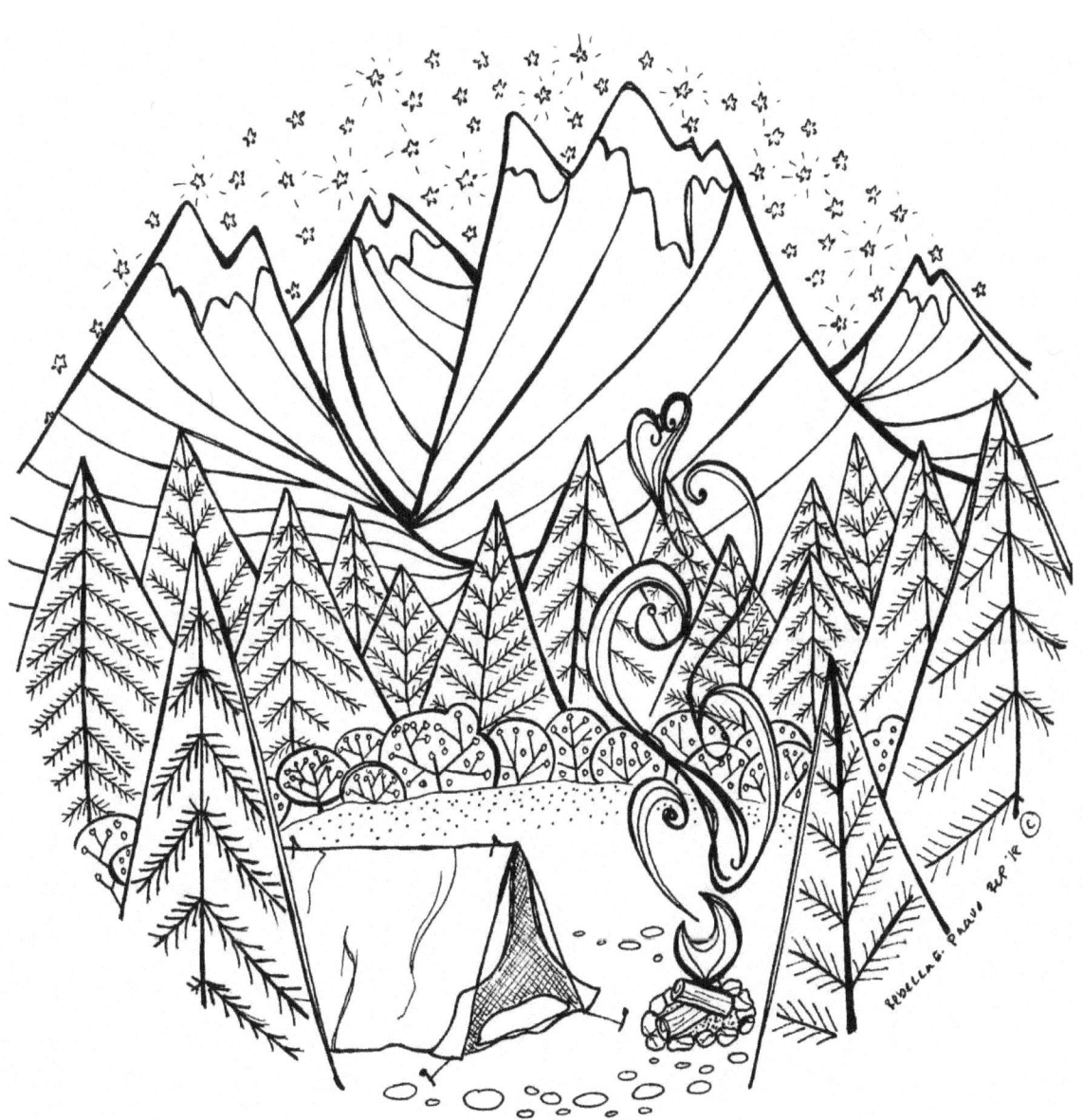

Rebecca Paavo© www.sorrelwoodstudio.com

Rebecca Paavo© www.sorrelwoodstudio.com

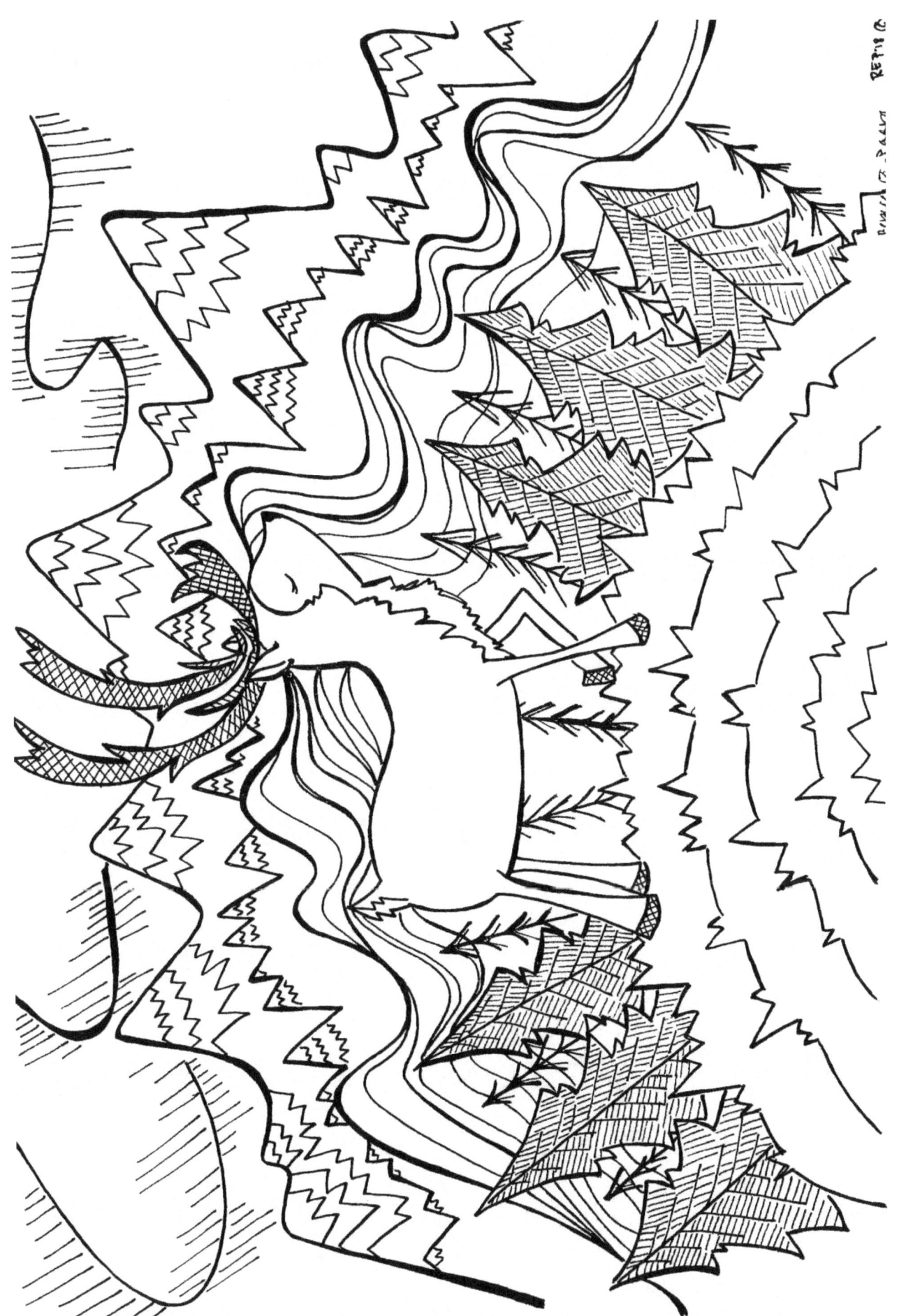

Rebecca Paavo© www.sorrelwoodstudio.com

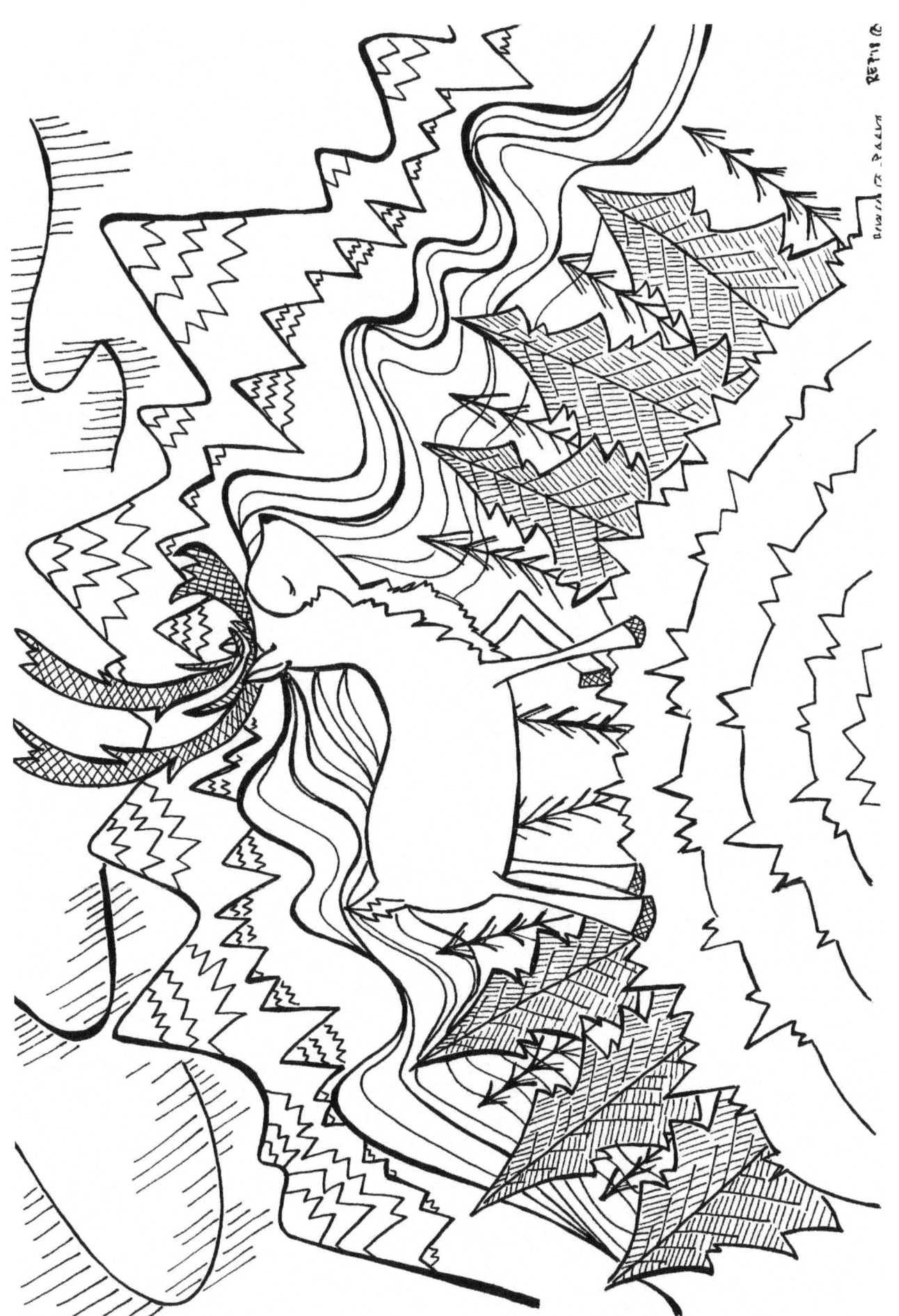

Rebecca Paavo© www.sorrelwoodstudio.com

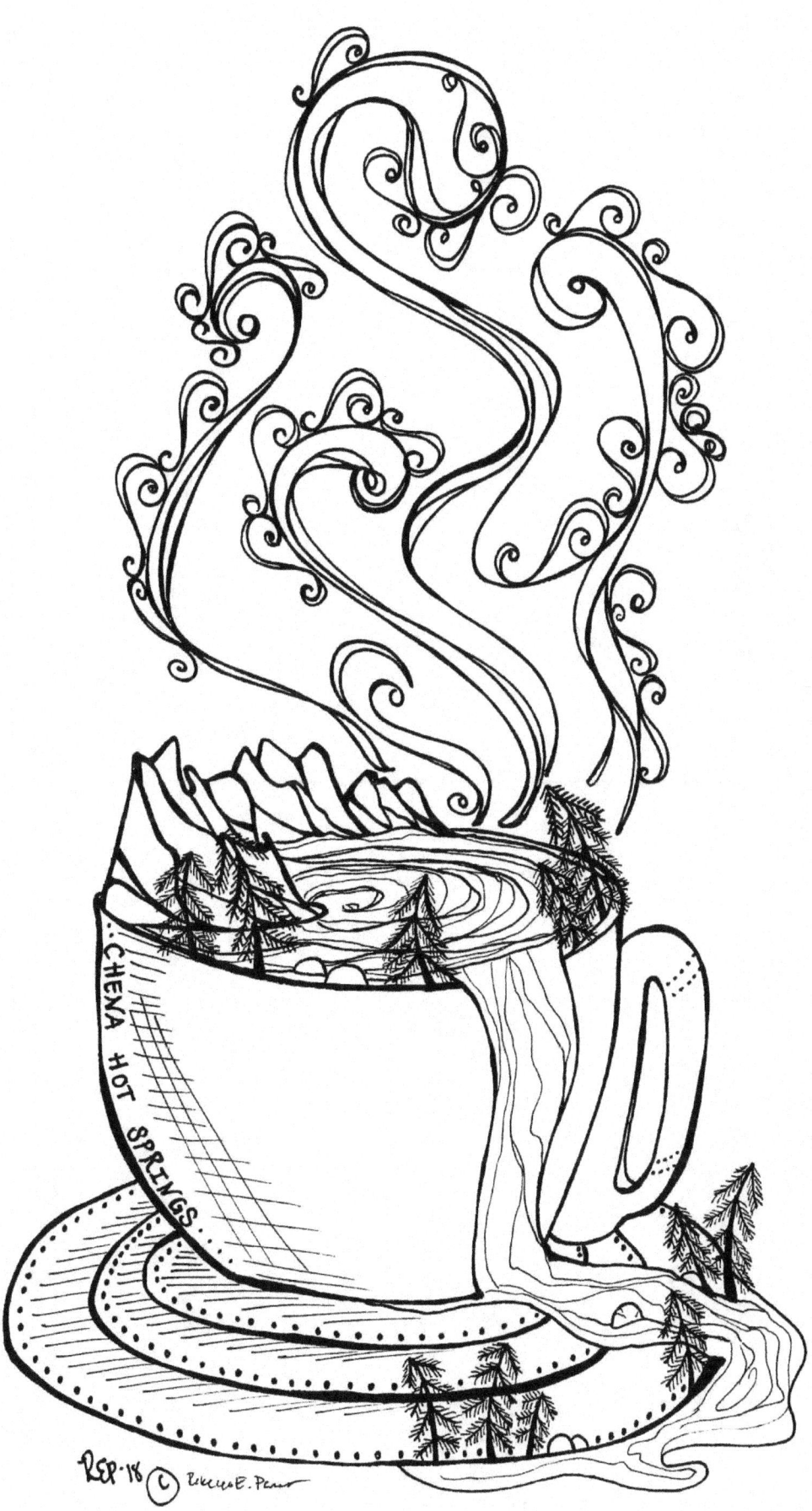

Rebecca Paavo© www.sorrelwoodstudio.com

Rebecca Paavo© www.sorrelwoodstudio.com

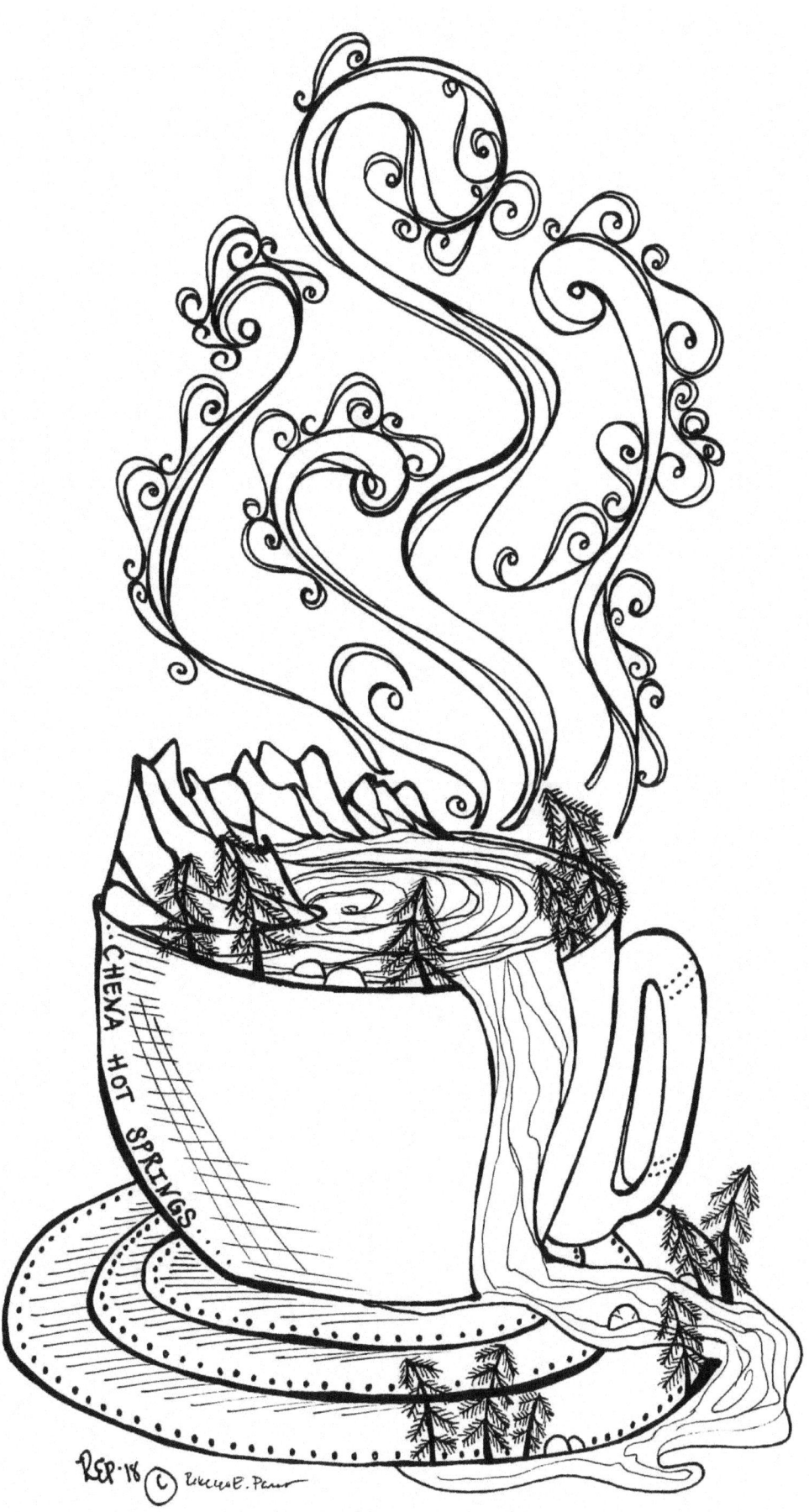

Rebecca Paavo© www.sorrelwoodstudio.com

Rebecca Paavo© www.sorrelwoodstudio.com

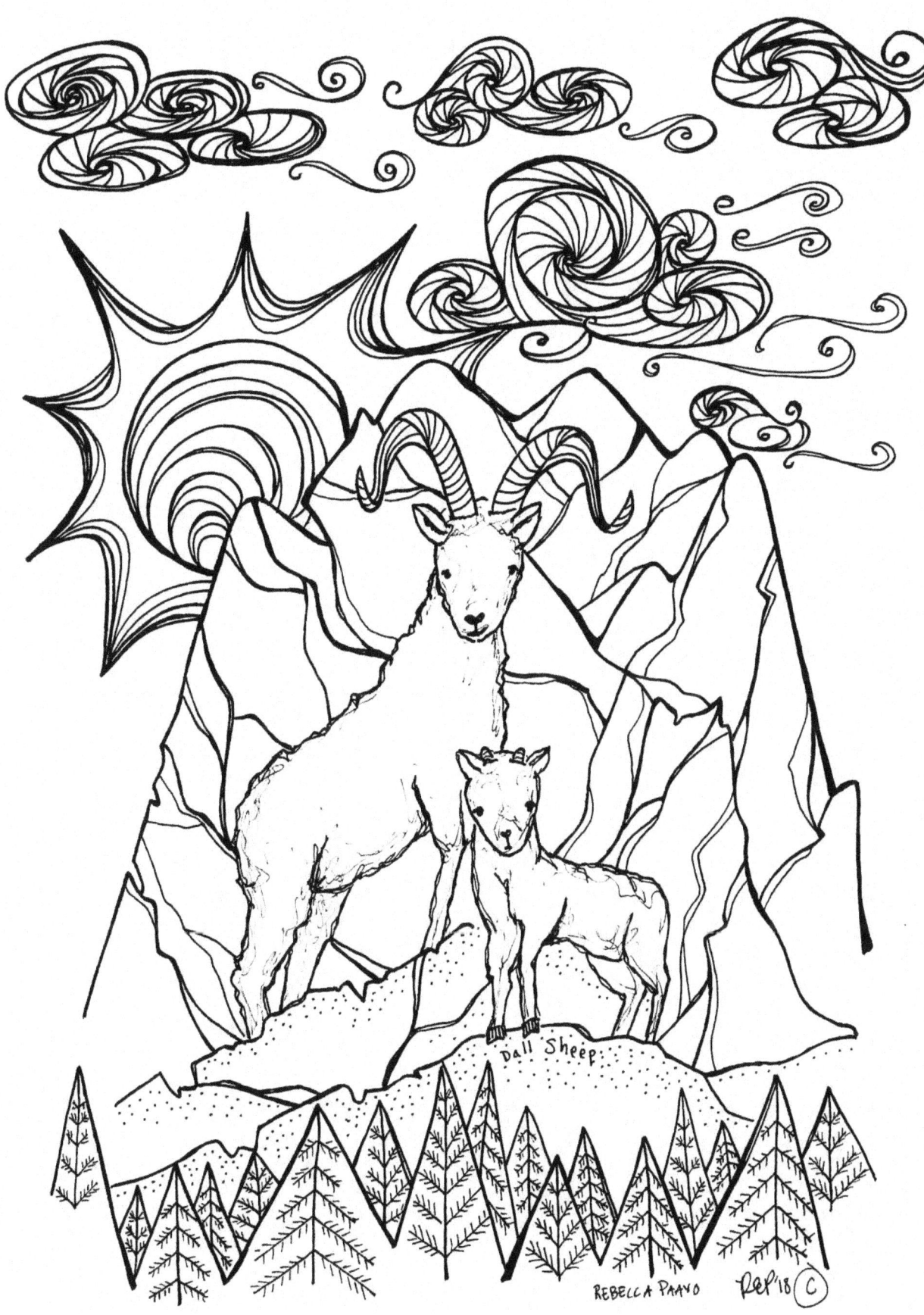

Rebecca Paavo© www.sorrelwoodstudio.com

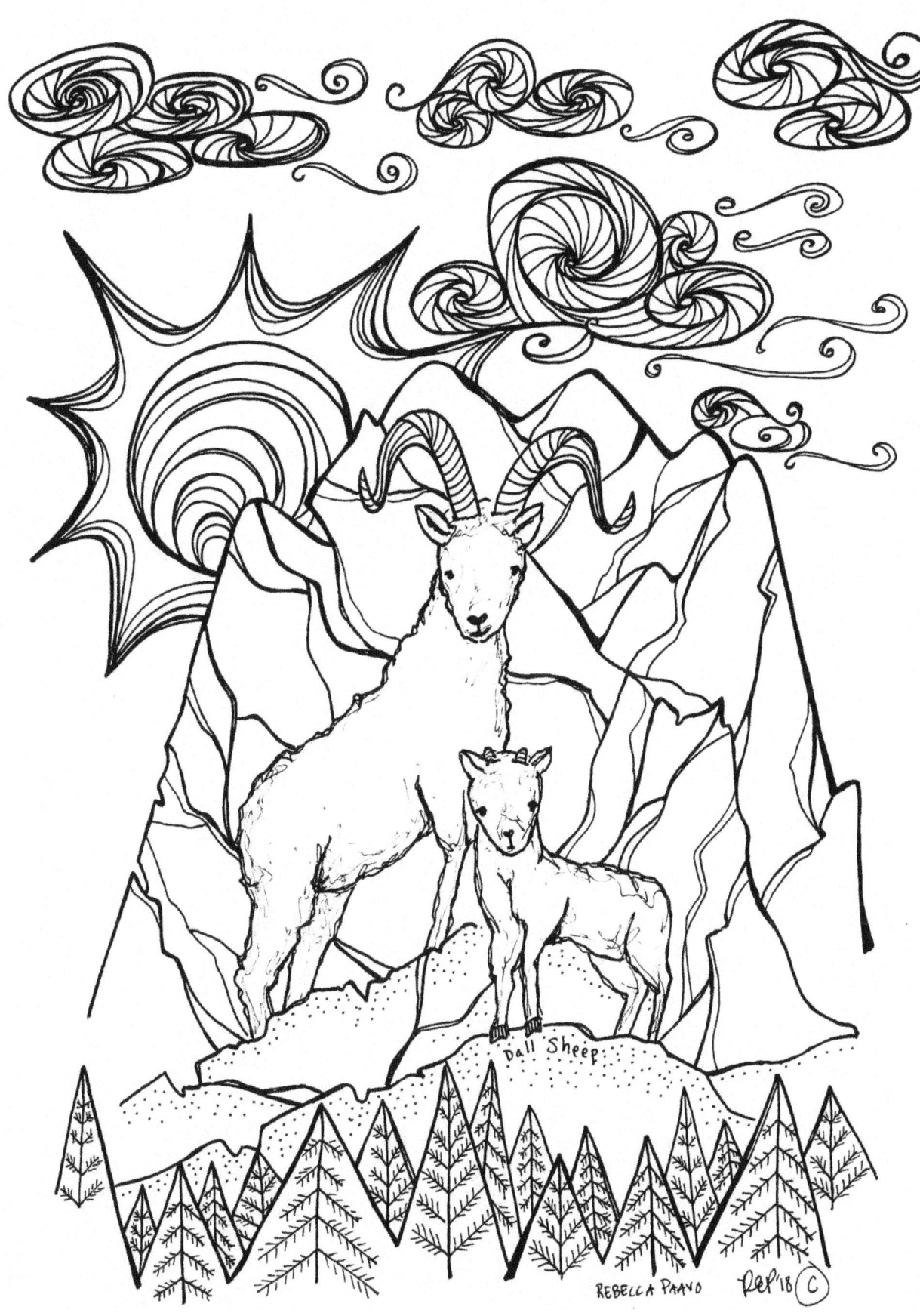

Rebecca Paavo© www.sorrelwoodstudio.com

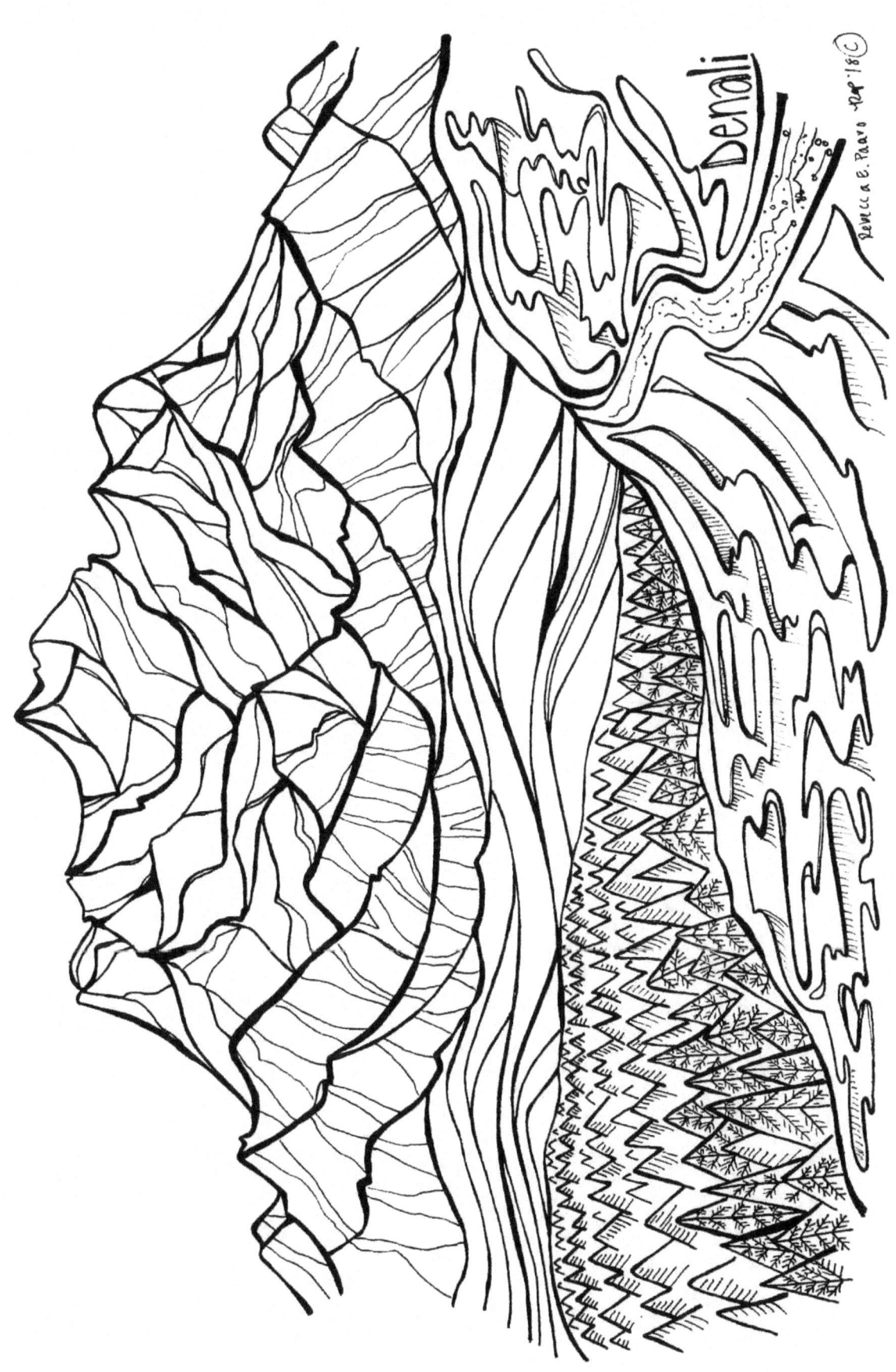

Rebecca Paavo© www.sorrelwoodstudio.com

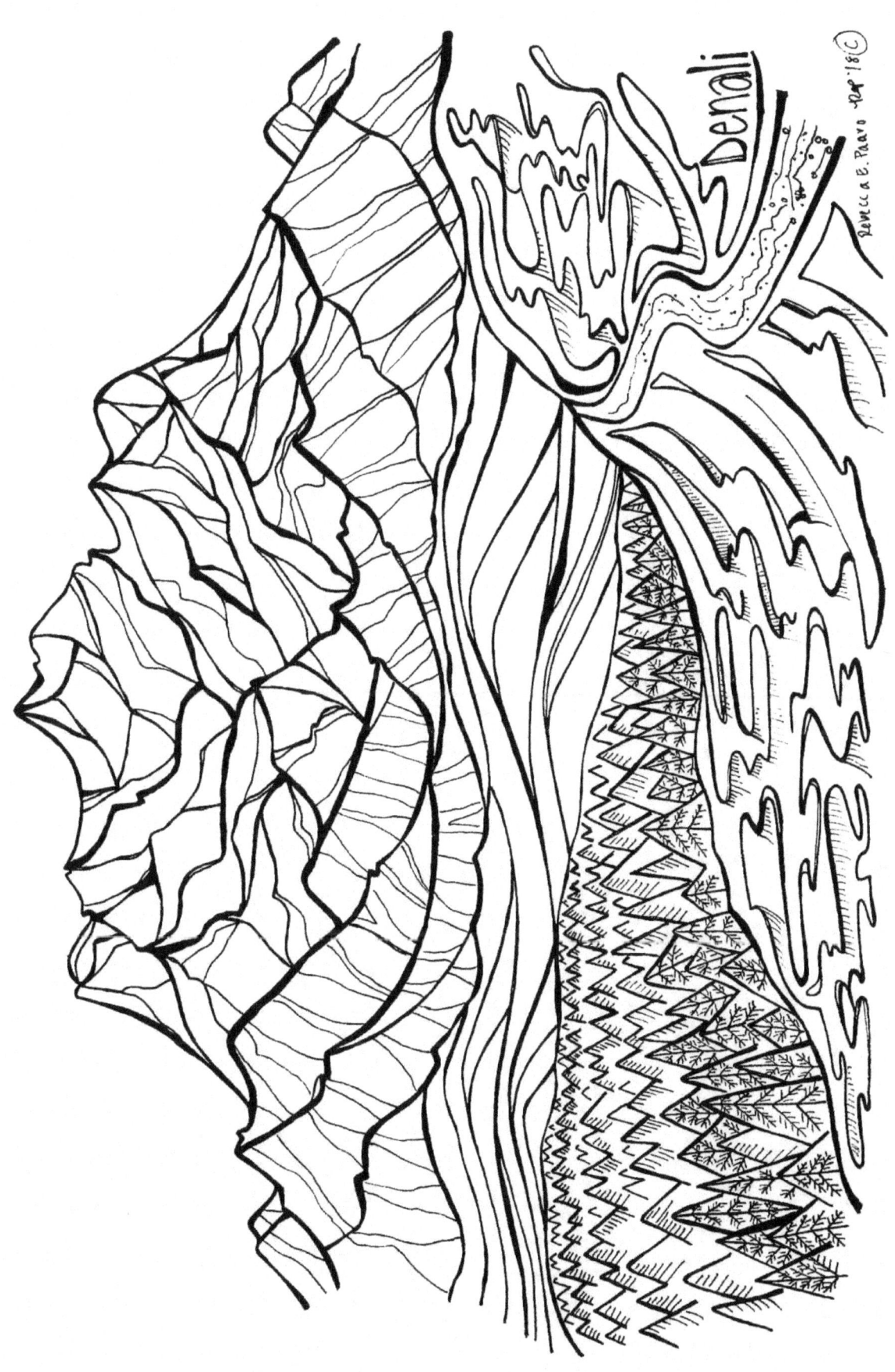

Rebecca Paavo© www.sorrelwoodstudio.com

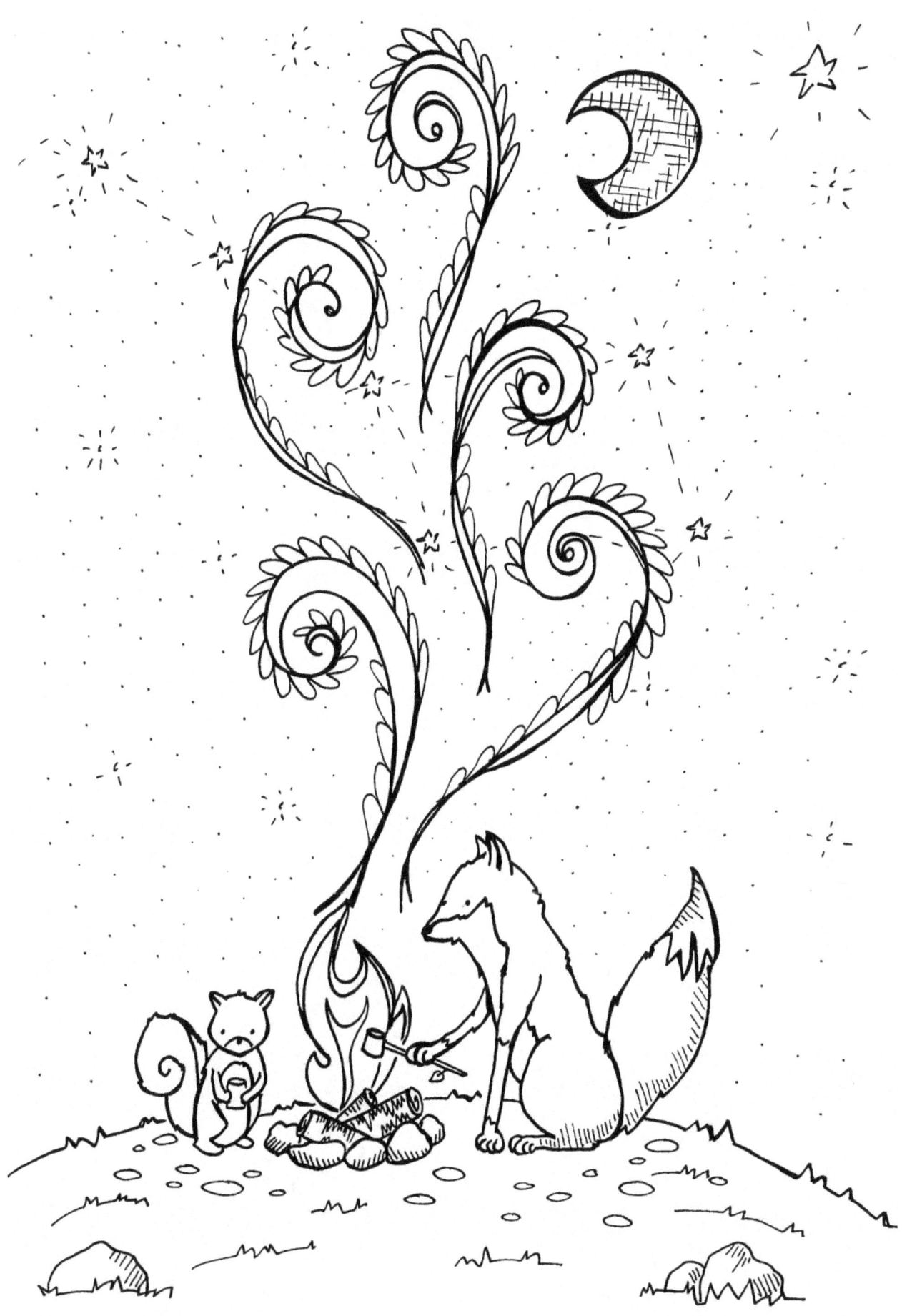

Rebecca Paavo© www.sorrelwoodstudio.com

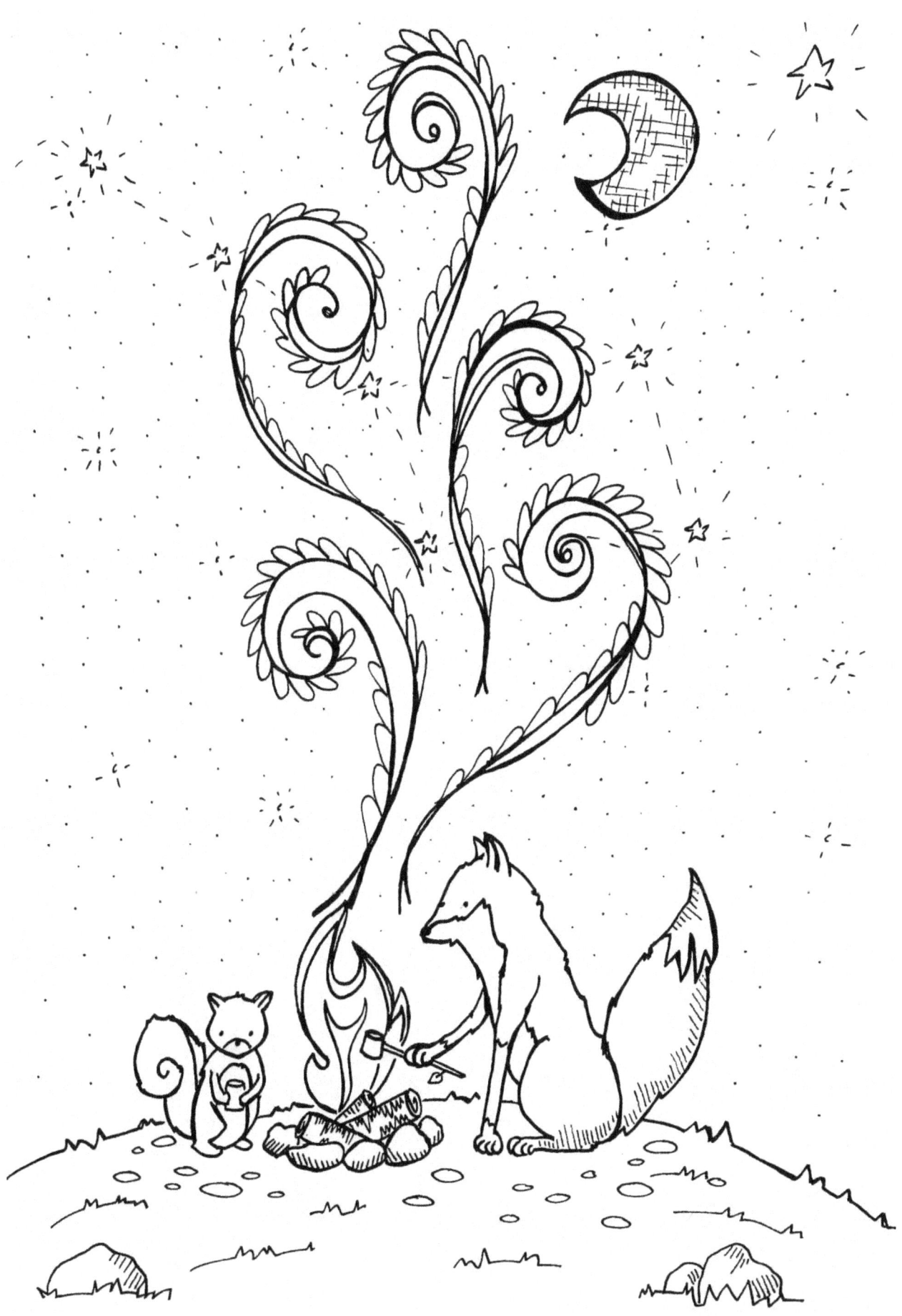

Rebecca Paavo© www.sorrelwoodstudio.com

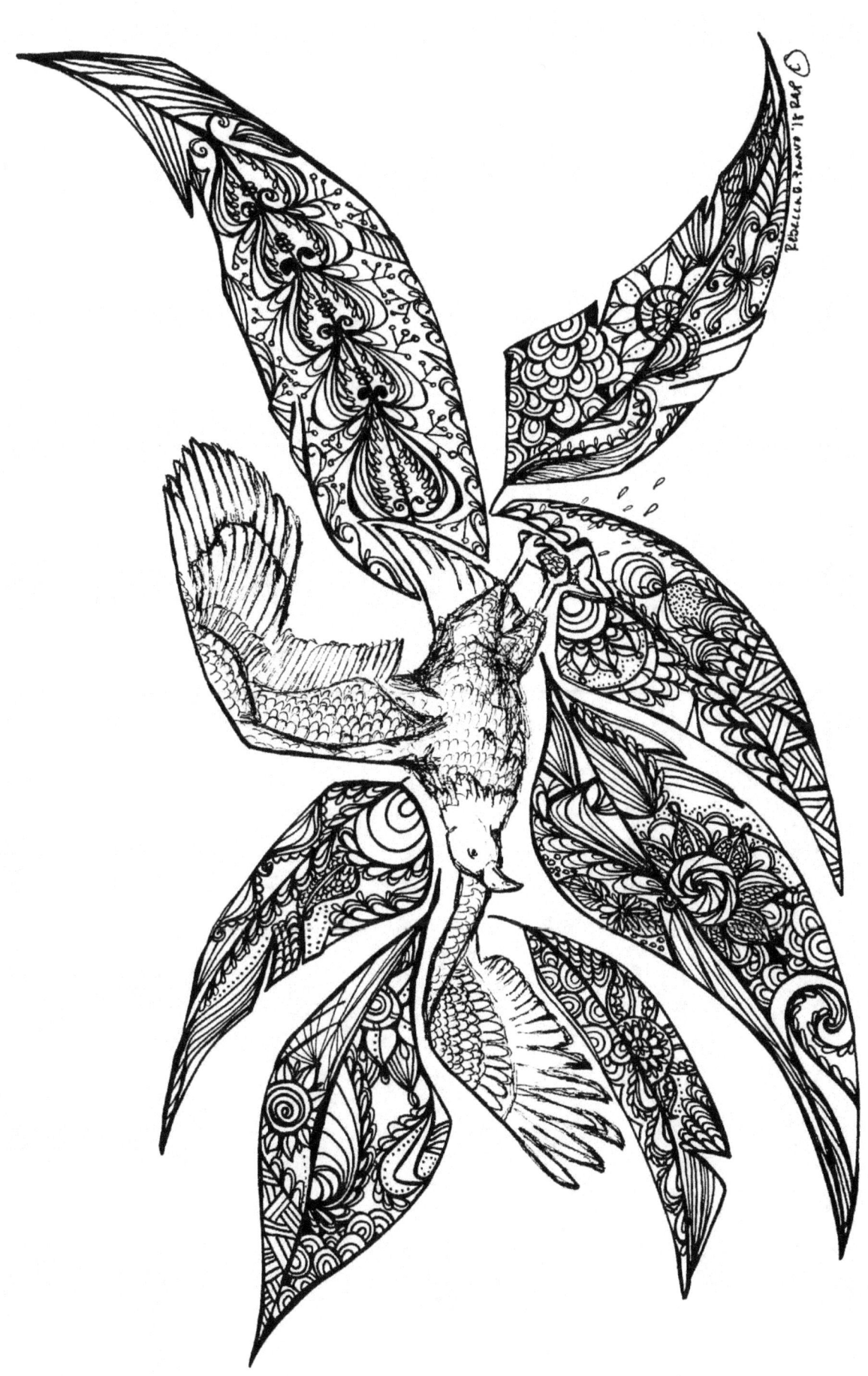

Rebecca Paavo© www.sorrelwoodstudio.com

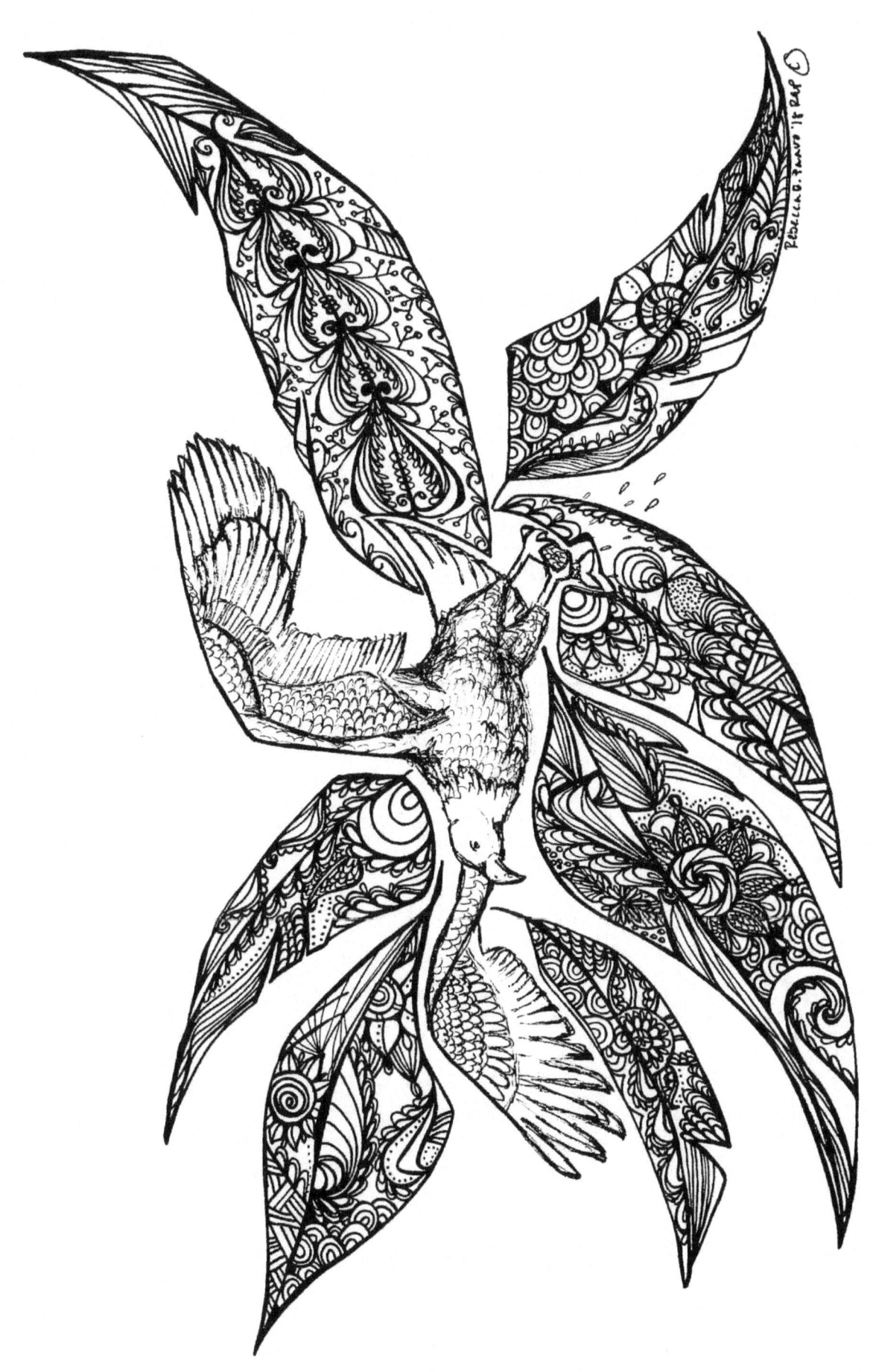

Rebecca Paavo© www.sorrelwoodstudio.com

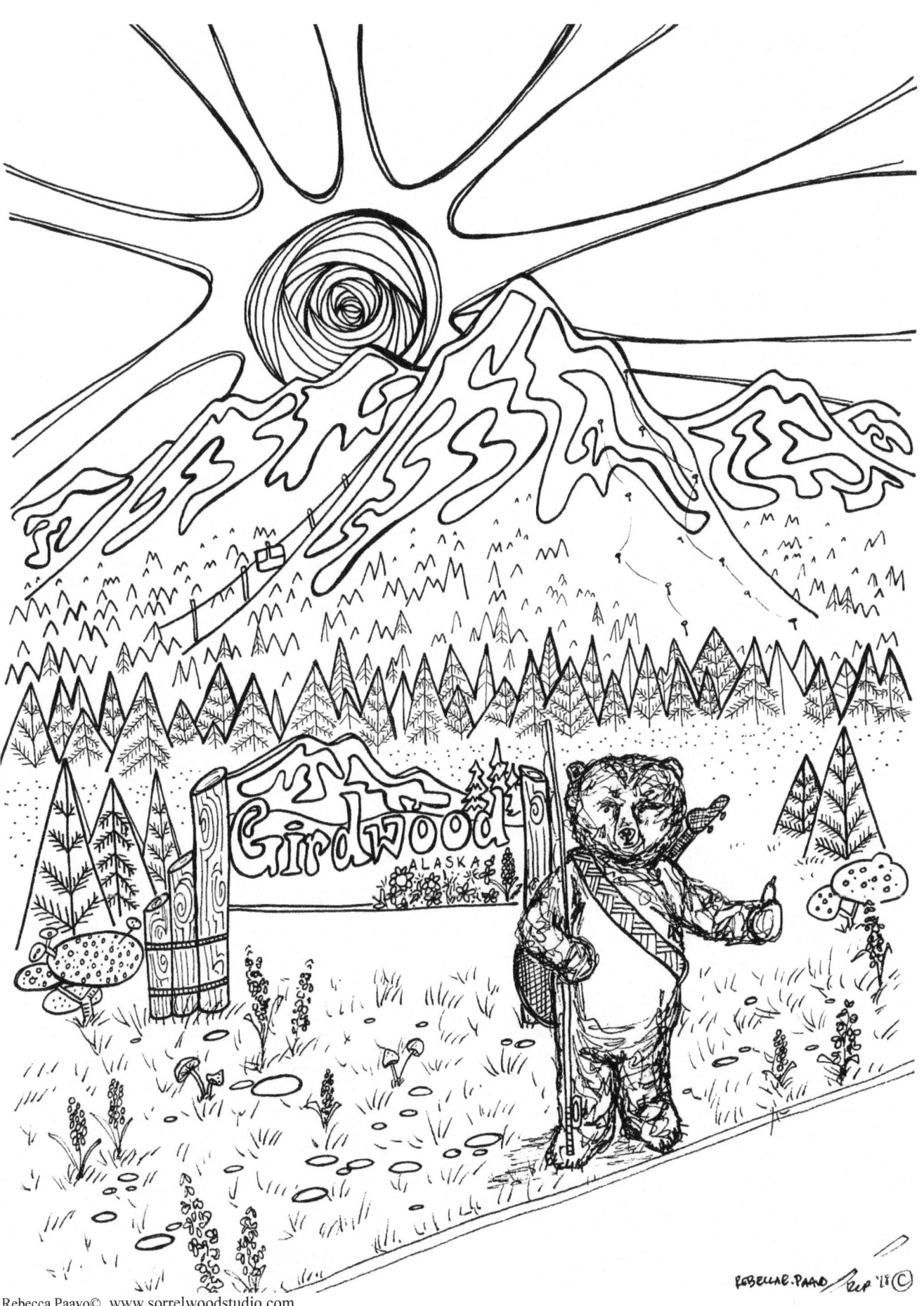

Rebecca Paavo© www.sorrelwoodstudio.com

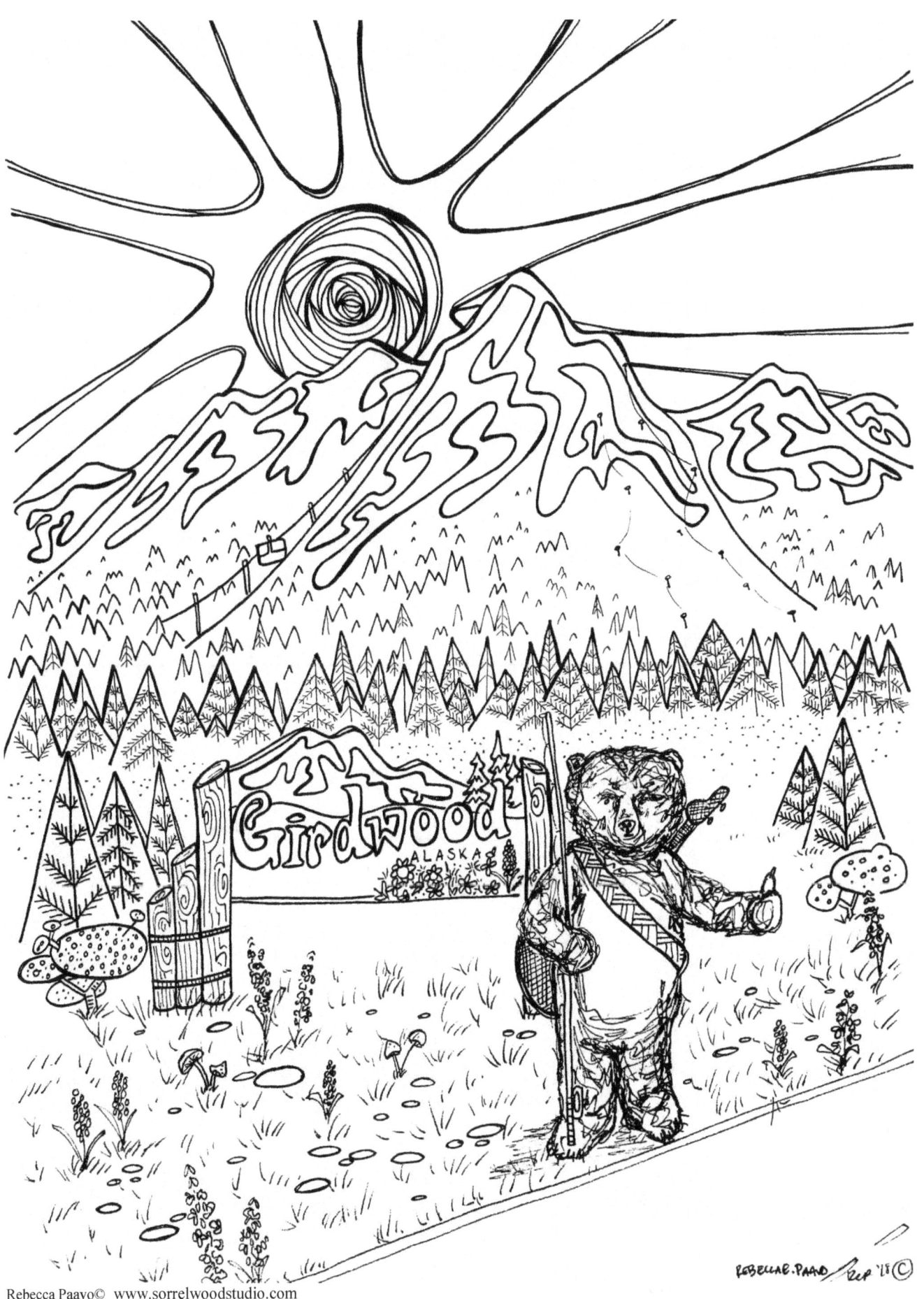

Rebecca Paavo© www.sorrelwoodstudio.com

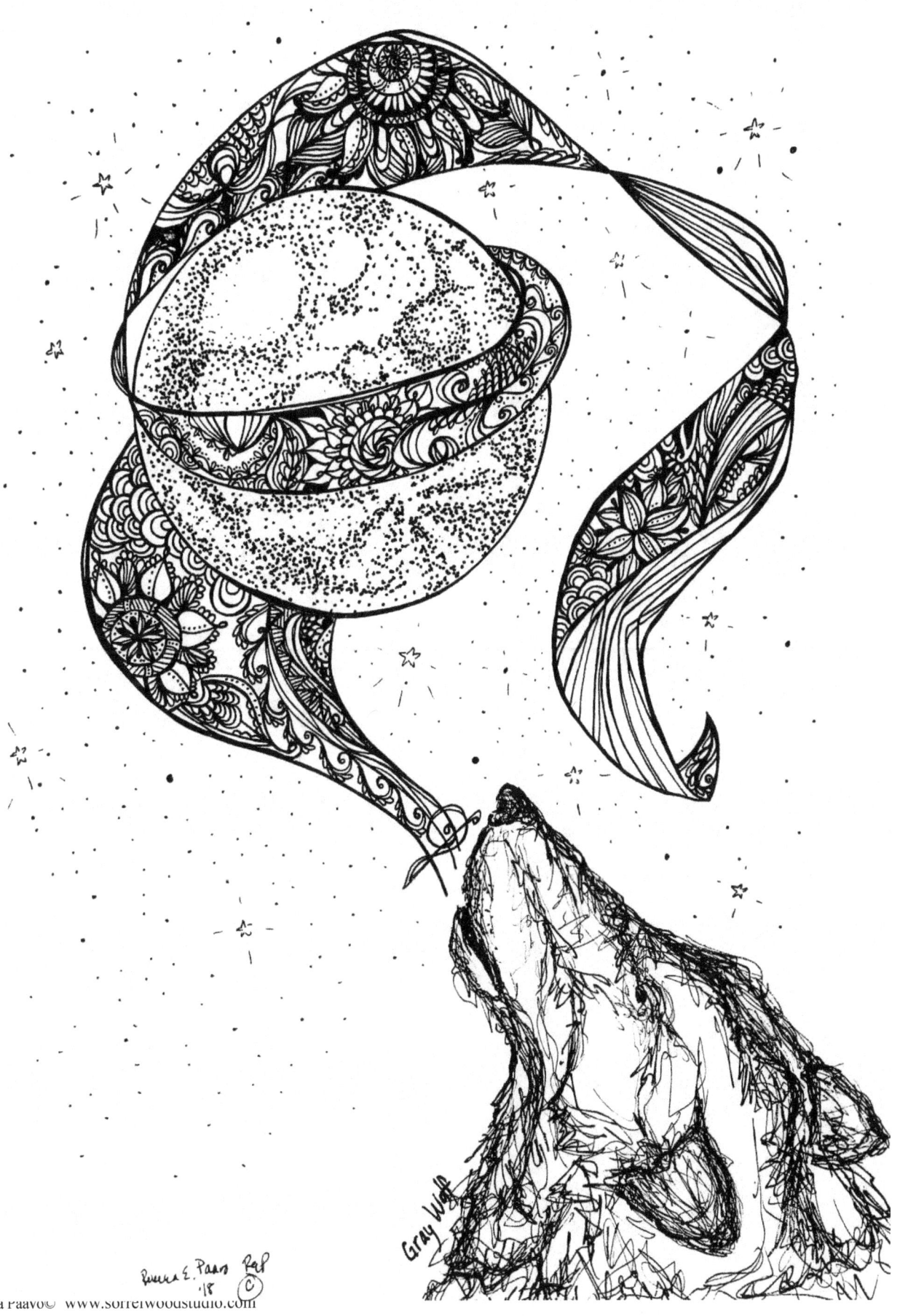

Rebecca Paavo© www.sorrelwoodstudio.com

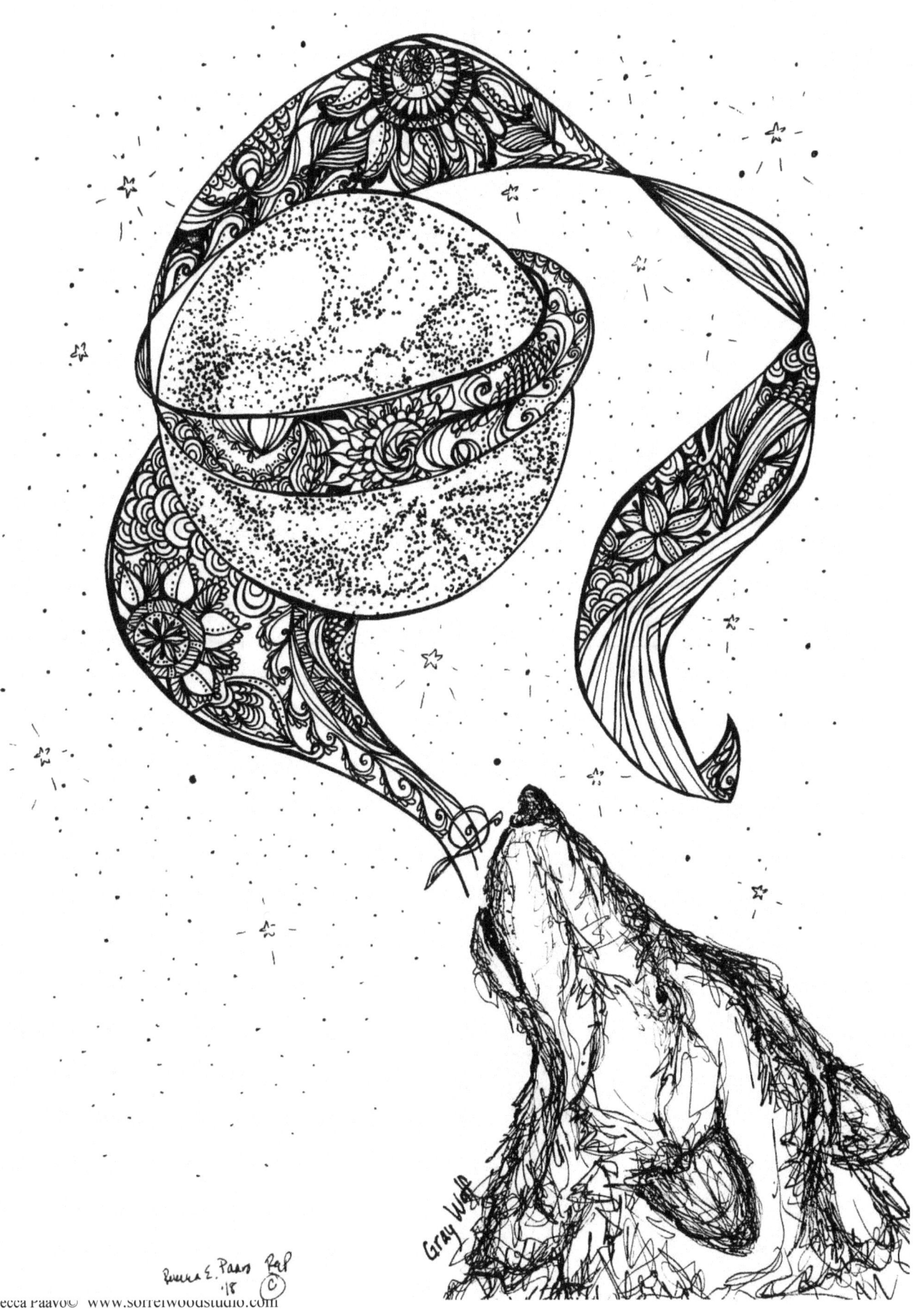

Rebecca Paavo© www.sorrelwoodstudio.com

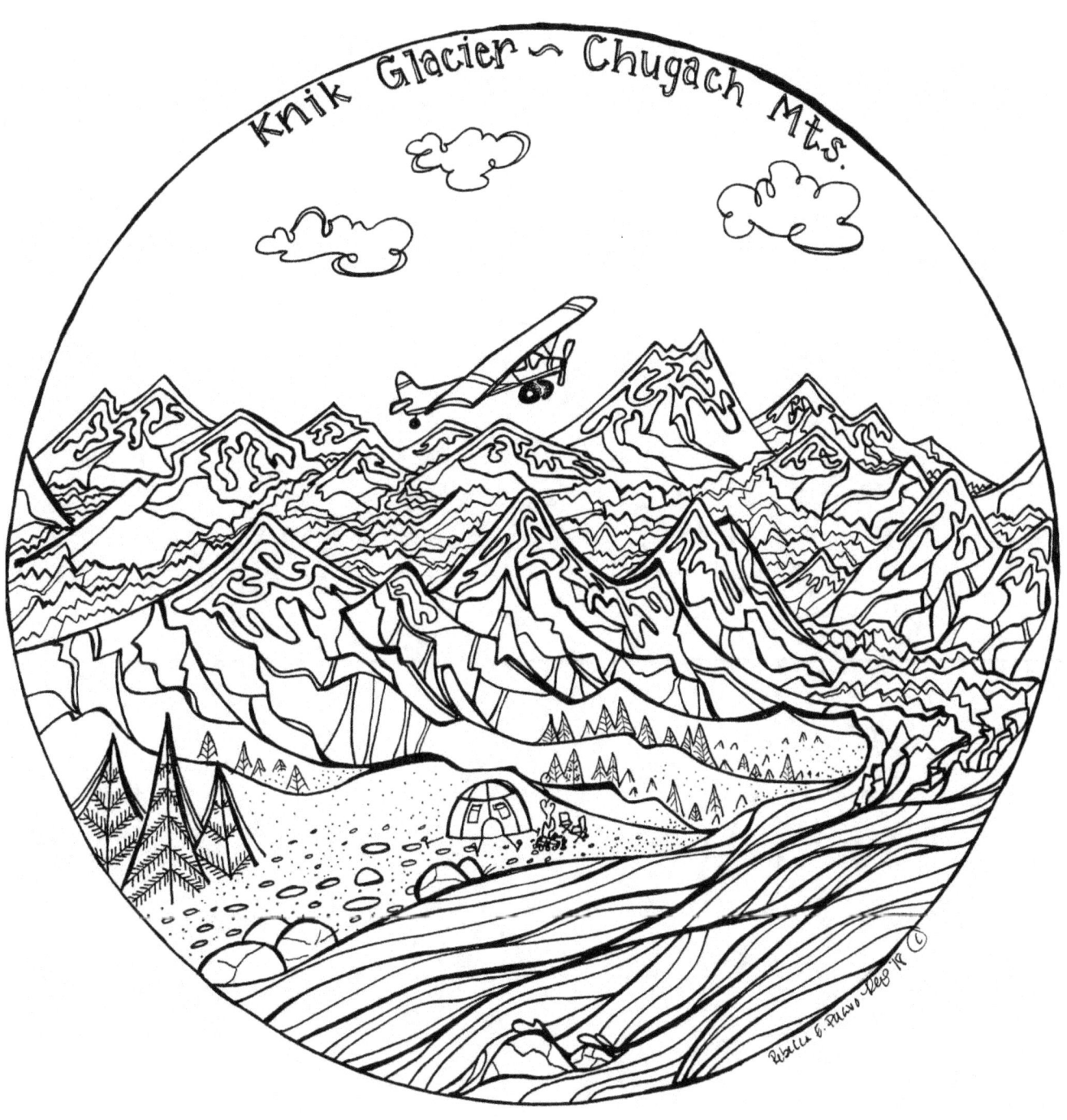

Rebecca Paavo© www.sorrelwoodstudio.com

Rebecca Paavo© www.sorrelwoodstudio.com

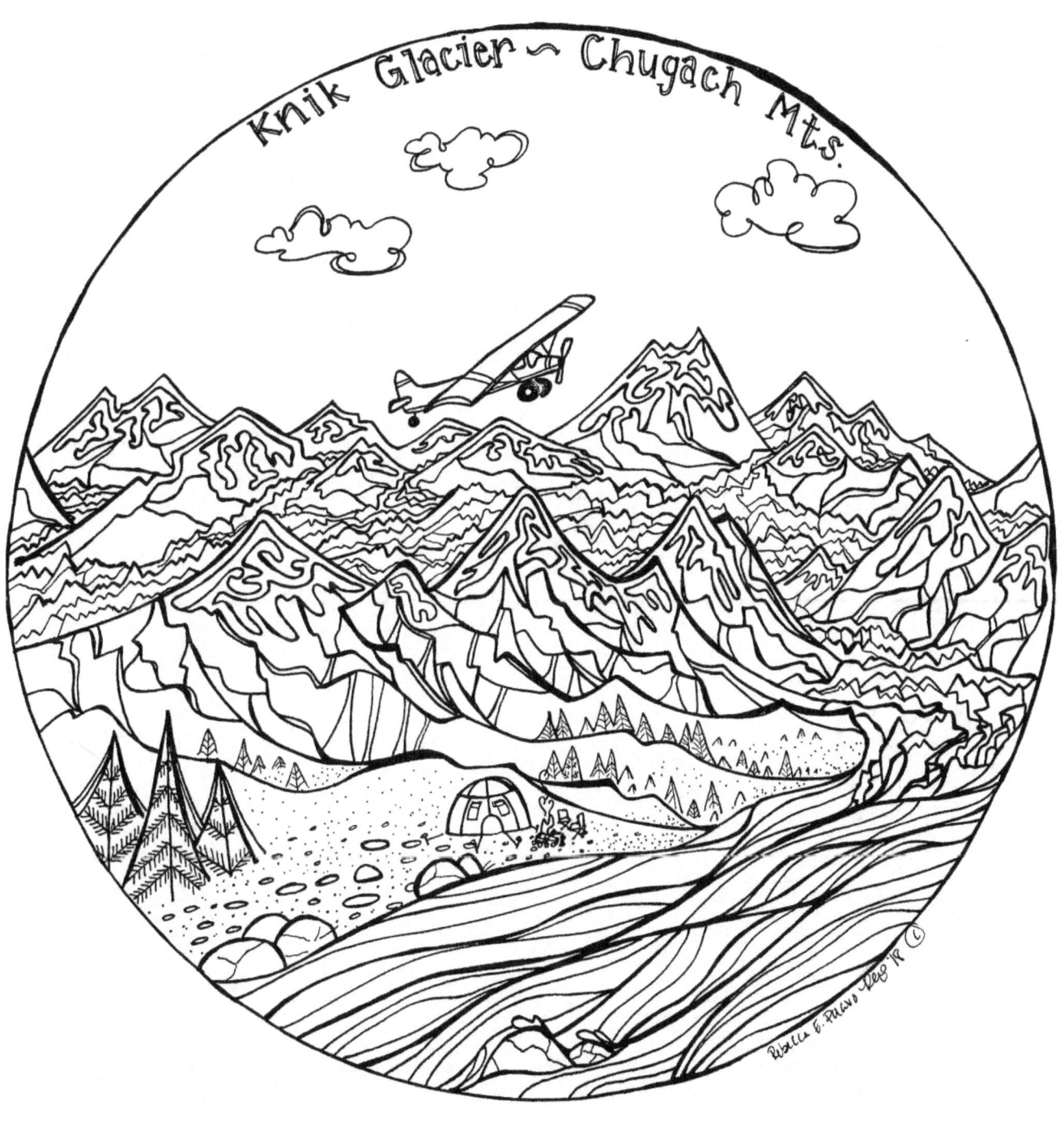

Rebecca Paavo© www.sorrelwoodstudio.com

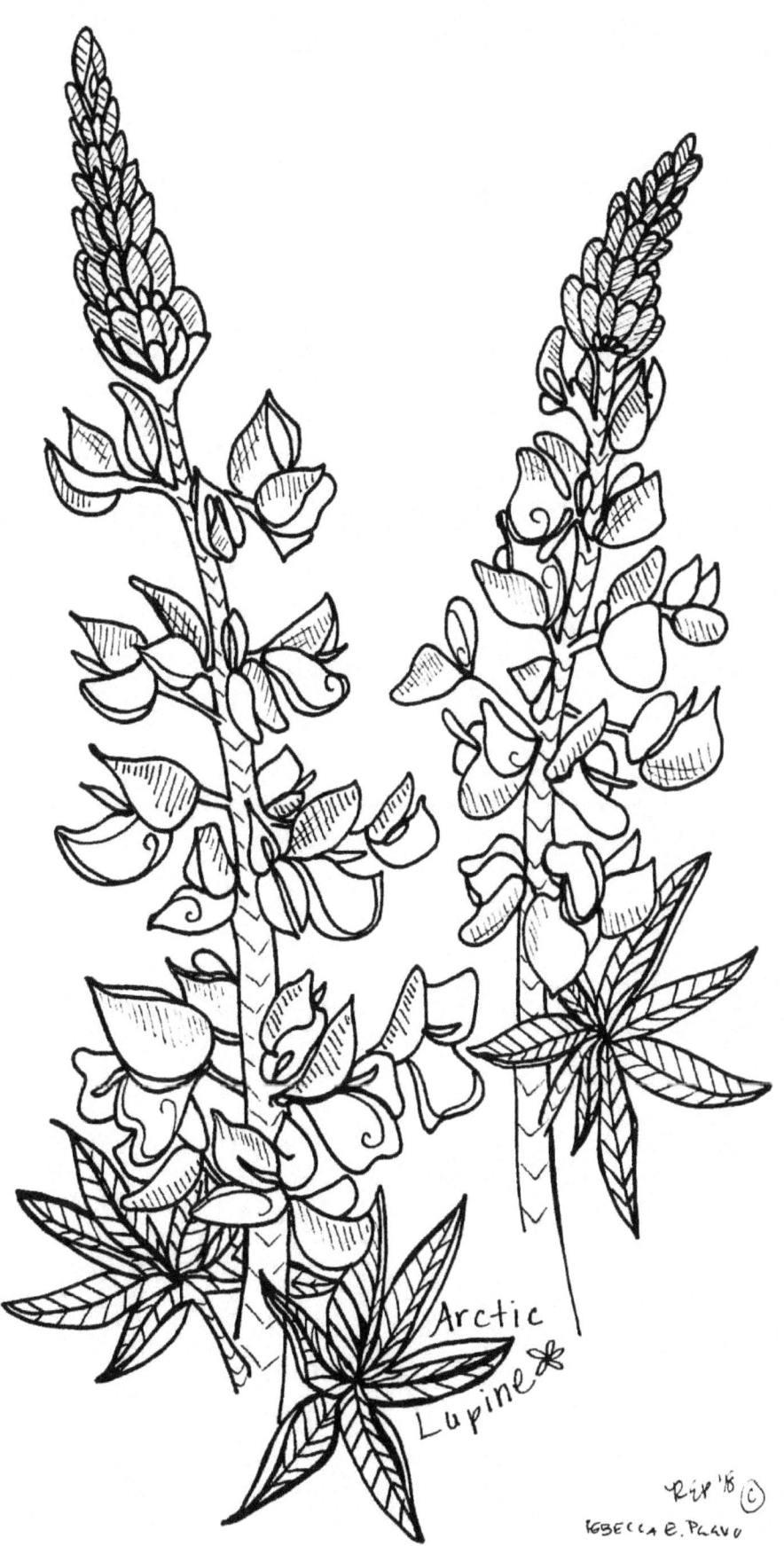

Rebecca Paavo© www.sorrelwoodstudio.com

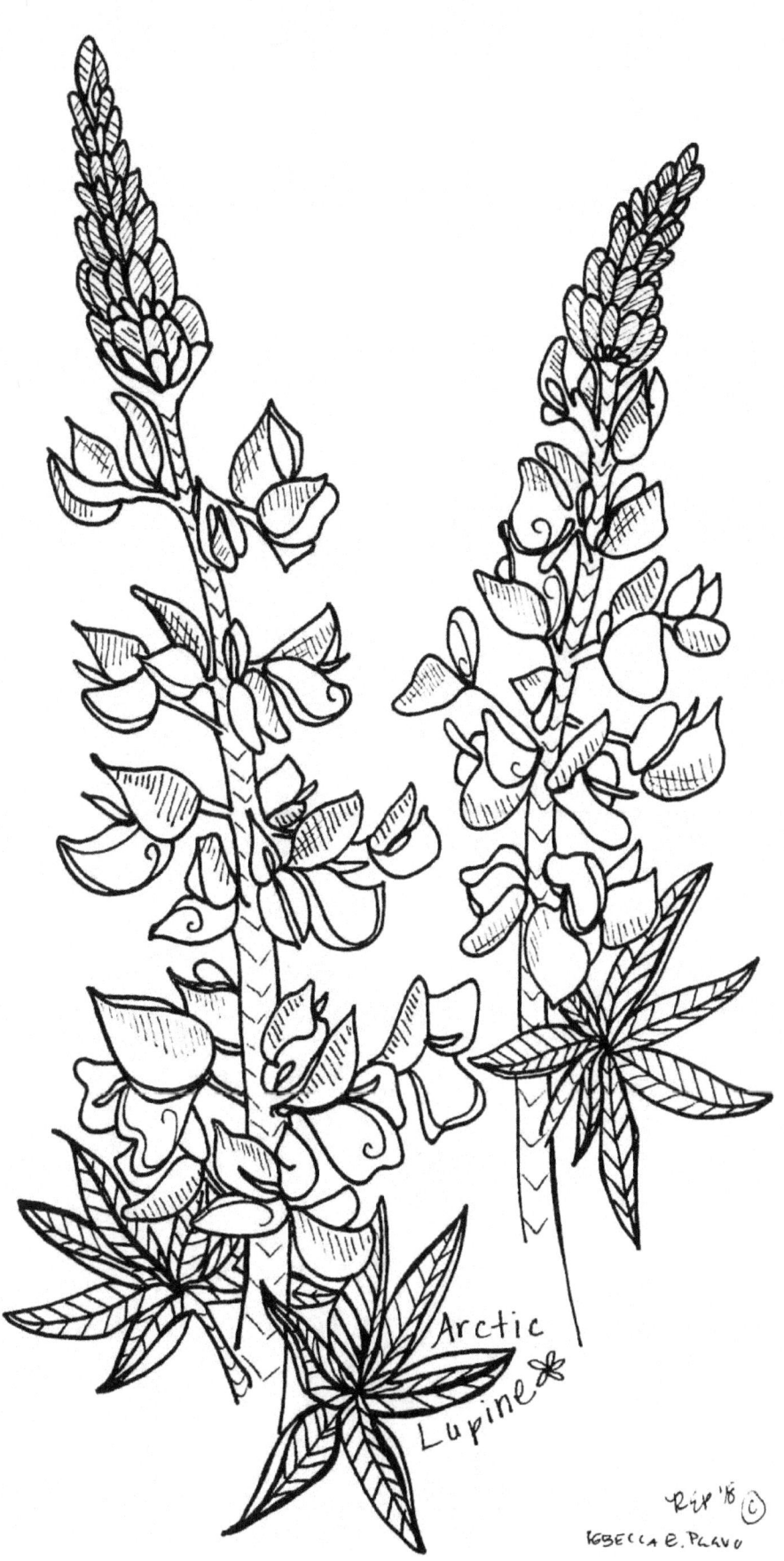

Rebecca Paavo© www.sorrelwoodstudio.com

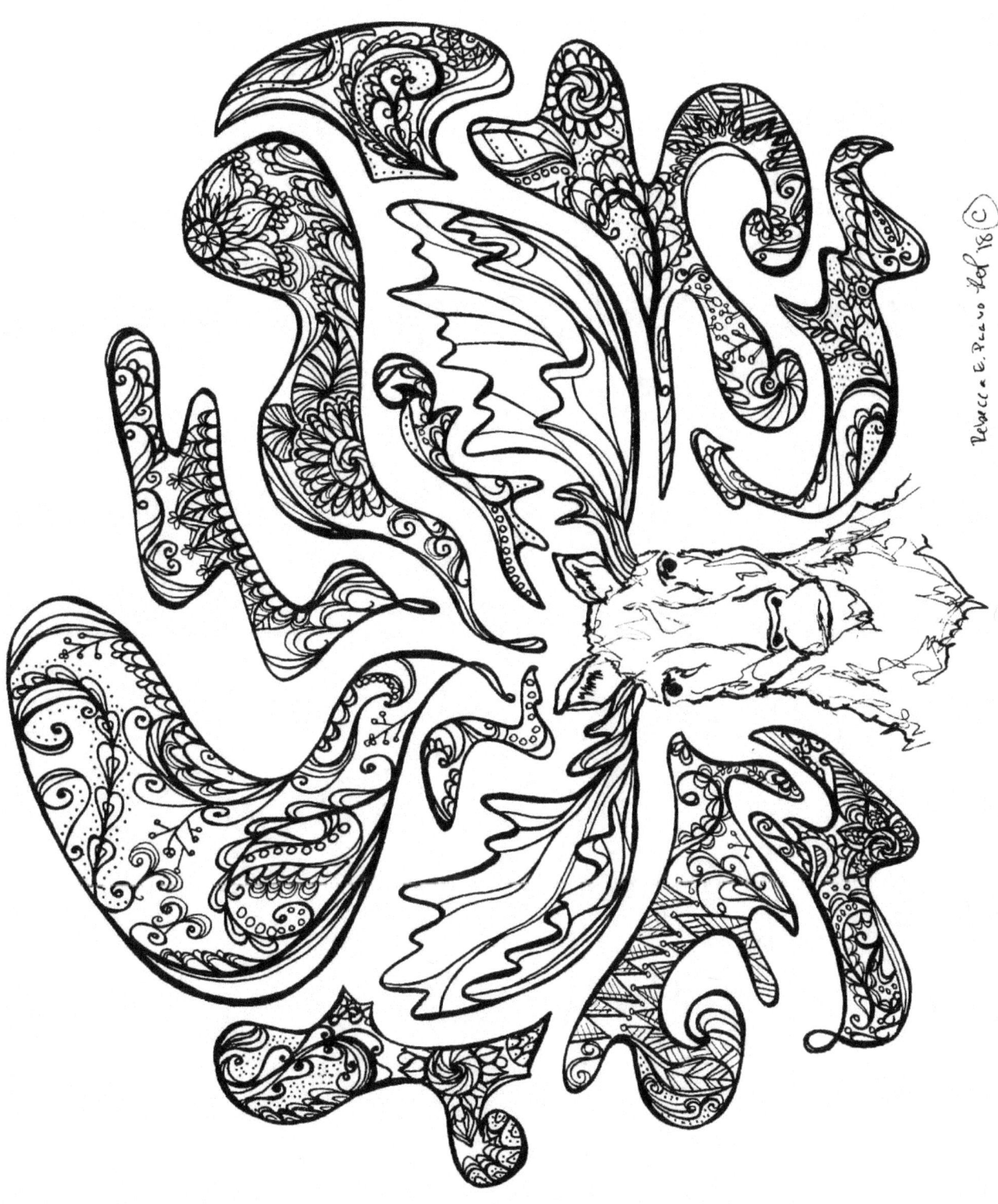

Rebecca Paavo© www.sorrelwoodstudio.com

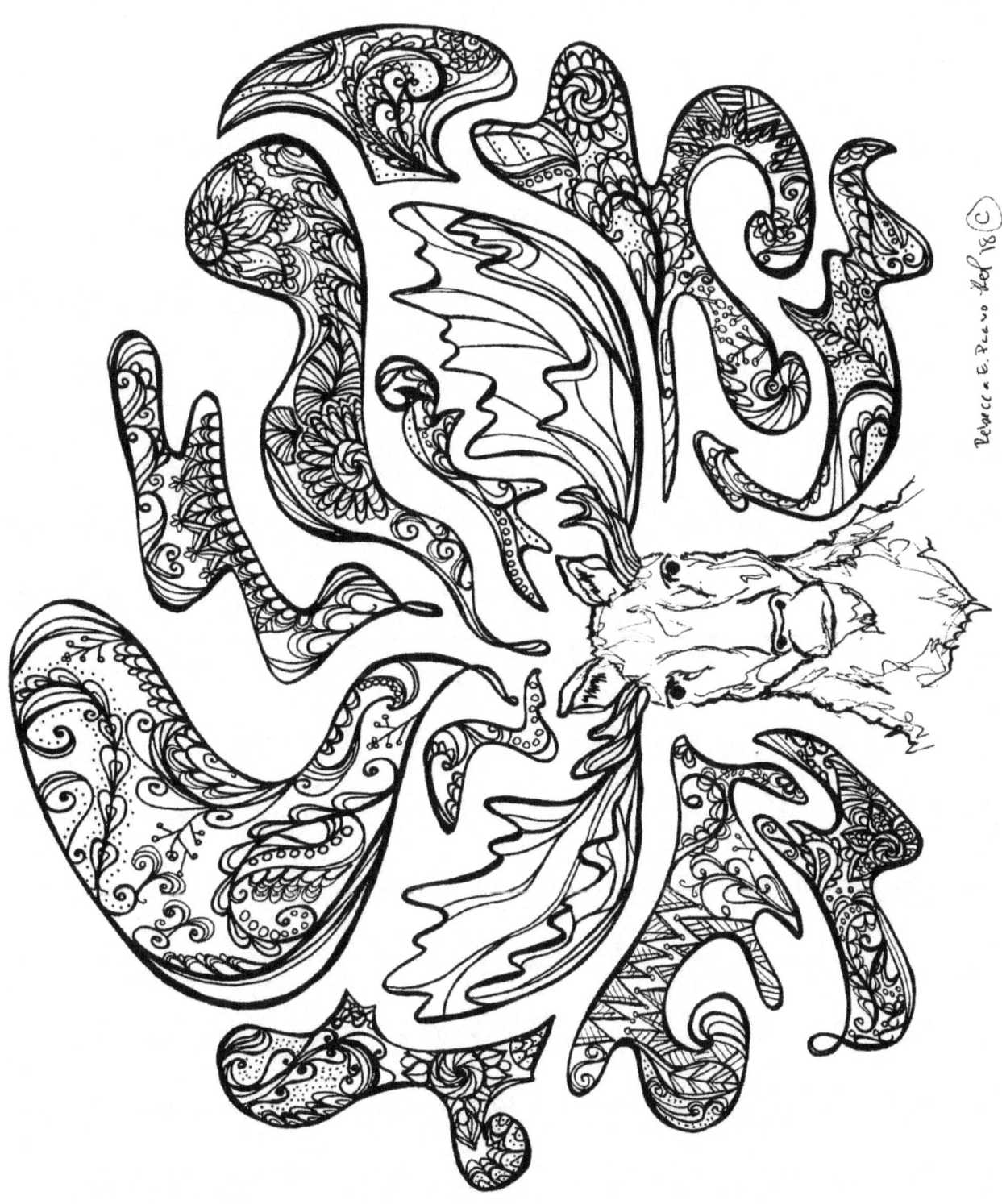

Rebecca Paavo© www.sorrelwoodstudio.com

Rebecca Paavo© www.sorrelwoodstudio.com

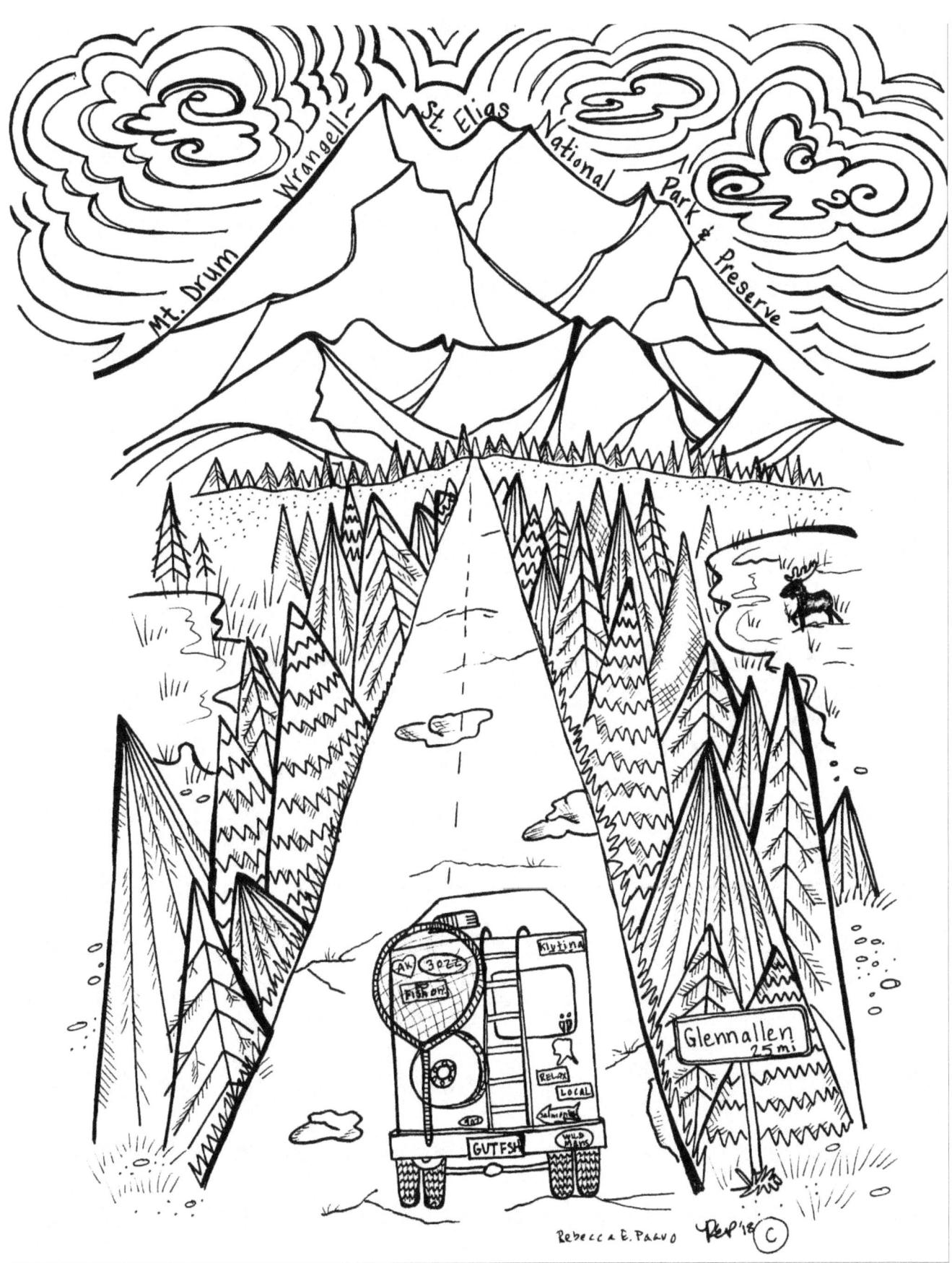

Rebecca Paavo© www.sorrelwoodstudio.com

Rebecca Paavo© www.sorrelwoodstudio.com

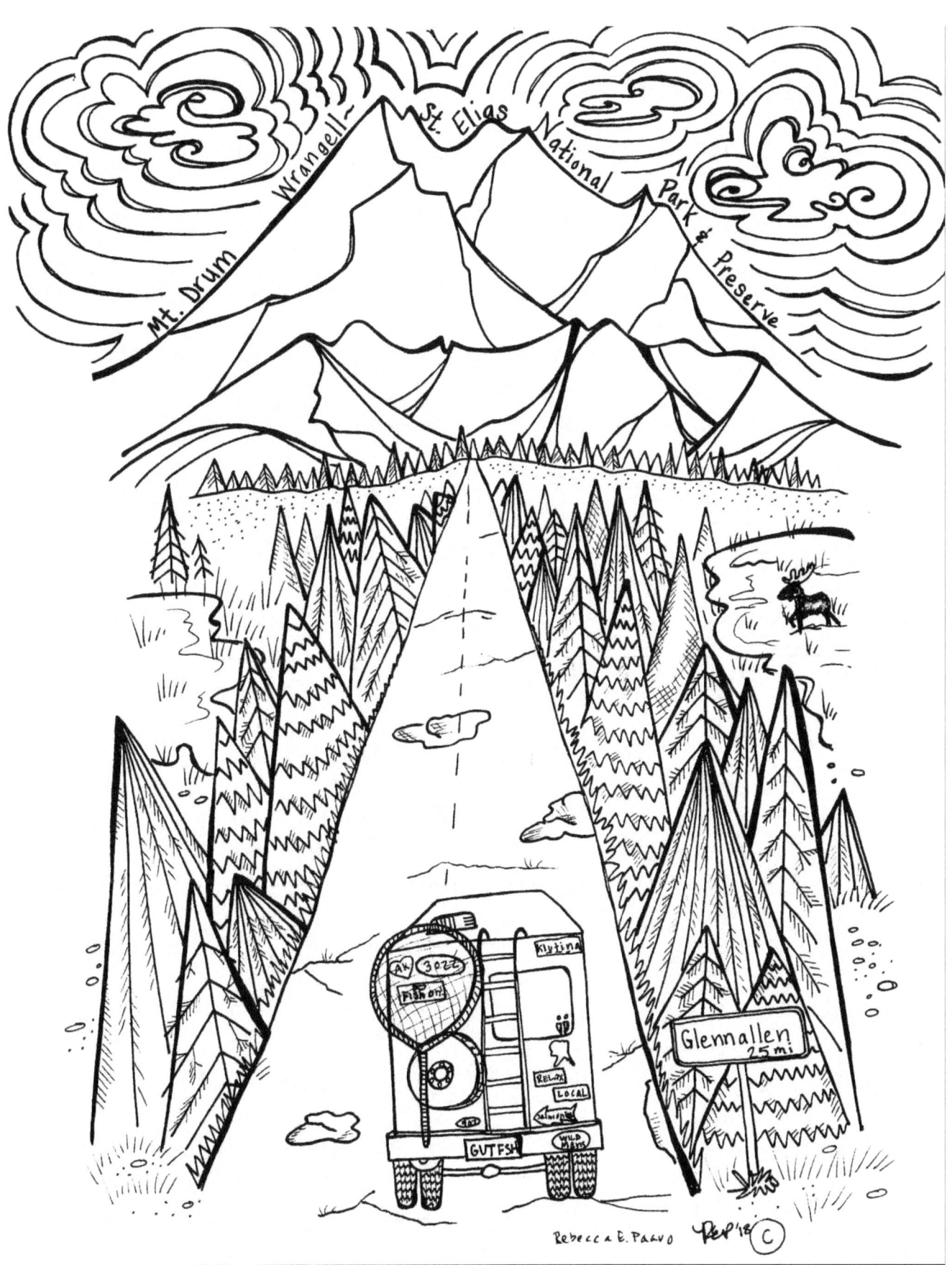

Rebecca Paavo© www.sorrelwoodstudio.com

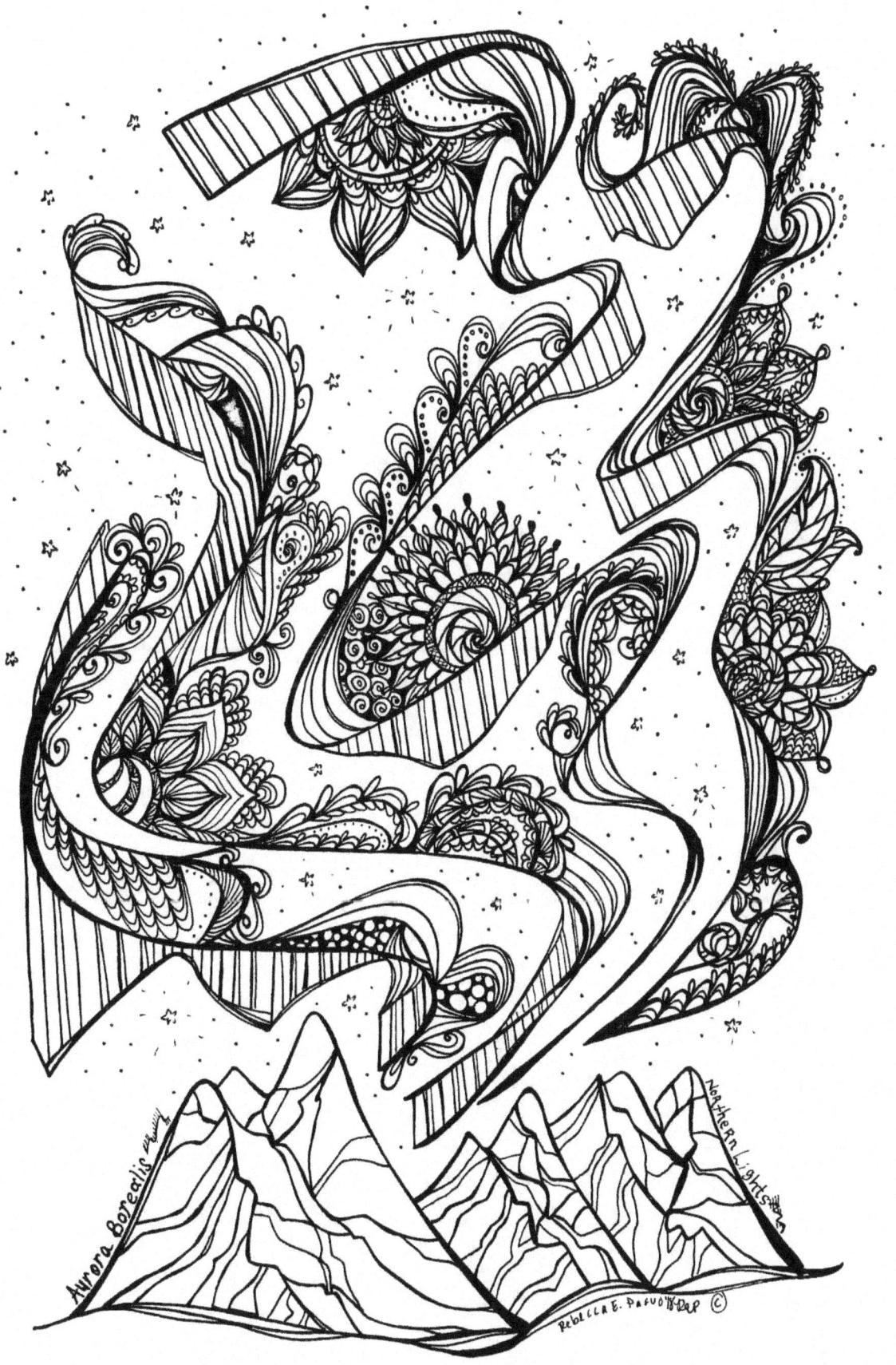

Rebecca Paavo© www.sorrelwoodstudio.com

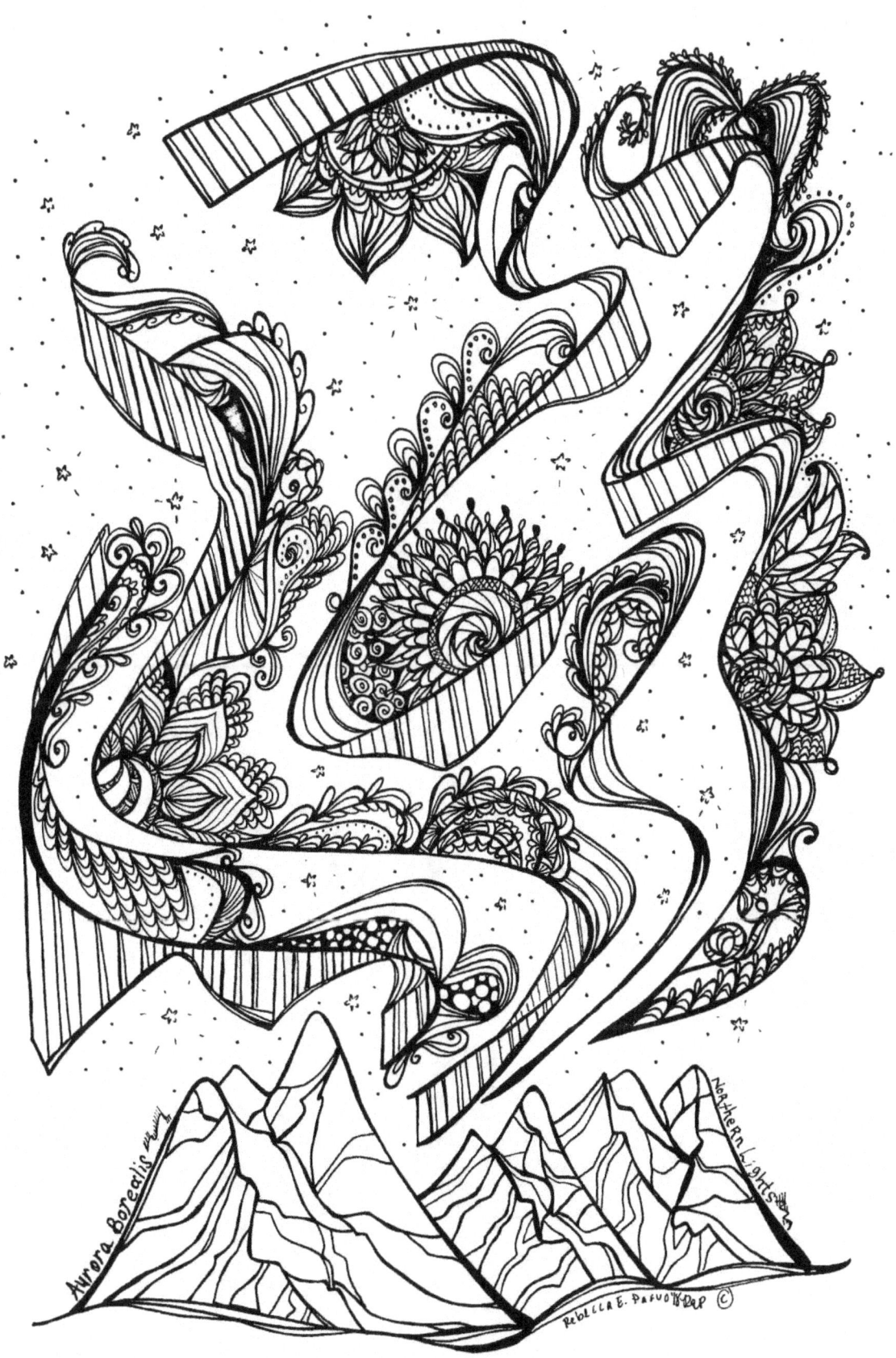

Rebecca Paavo© www.sorrelwoodstudio.com

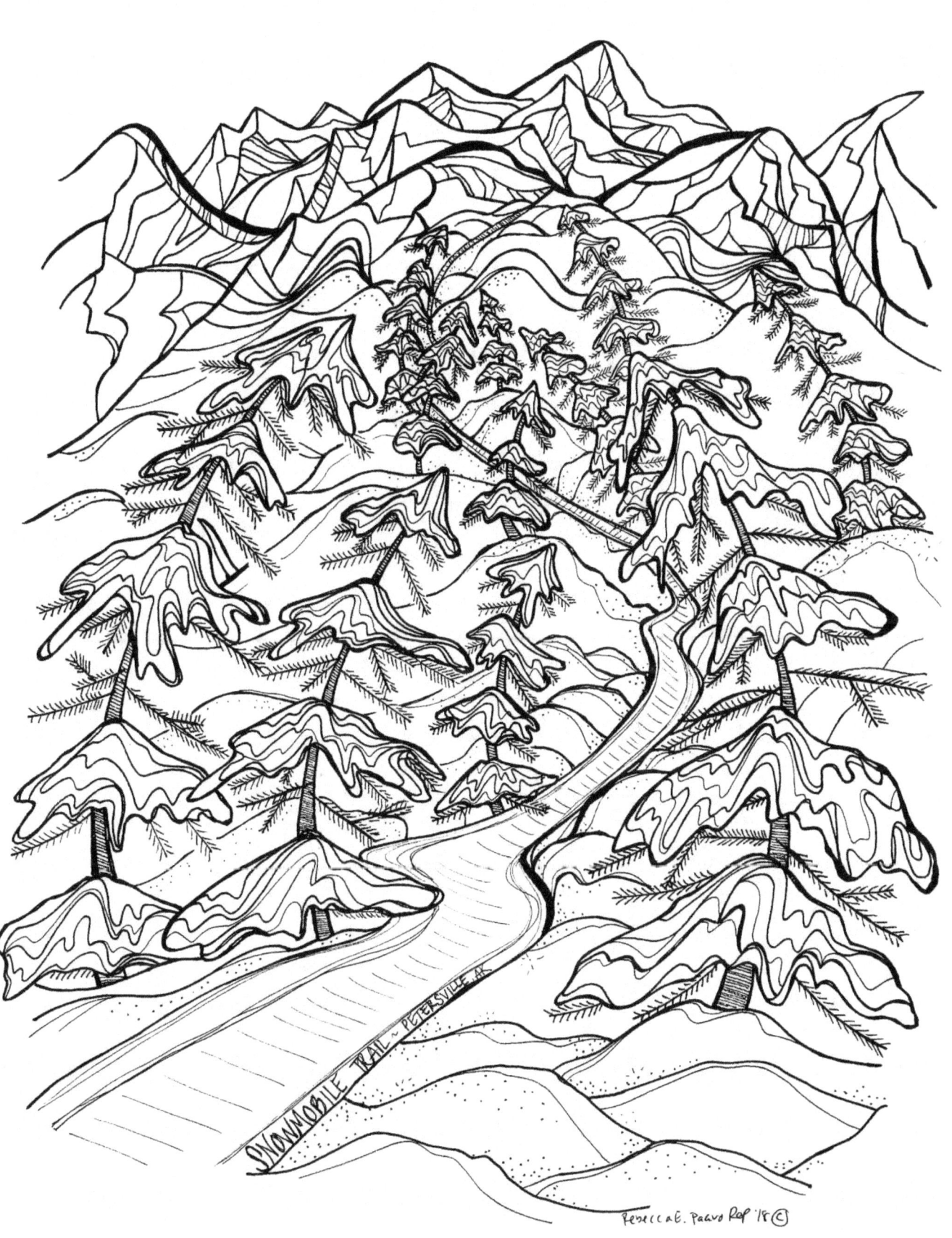

Rebecca Paavo© www.sorrelwoodstudio.com

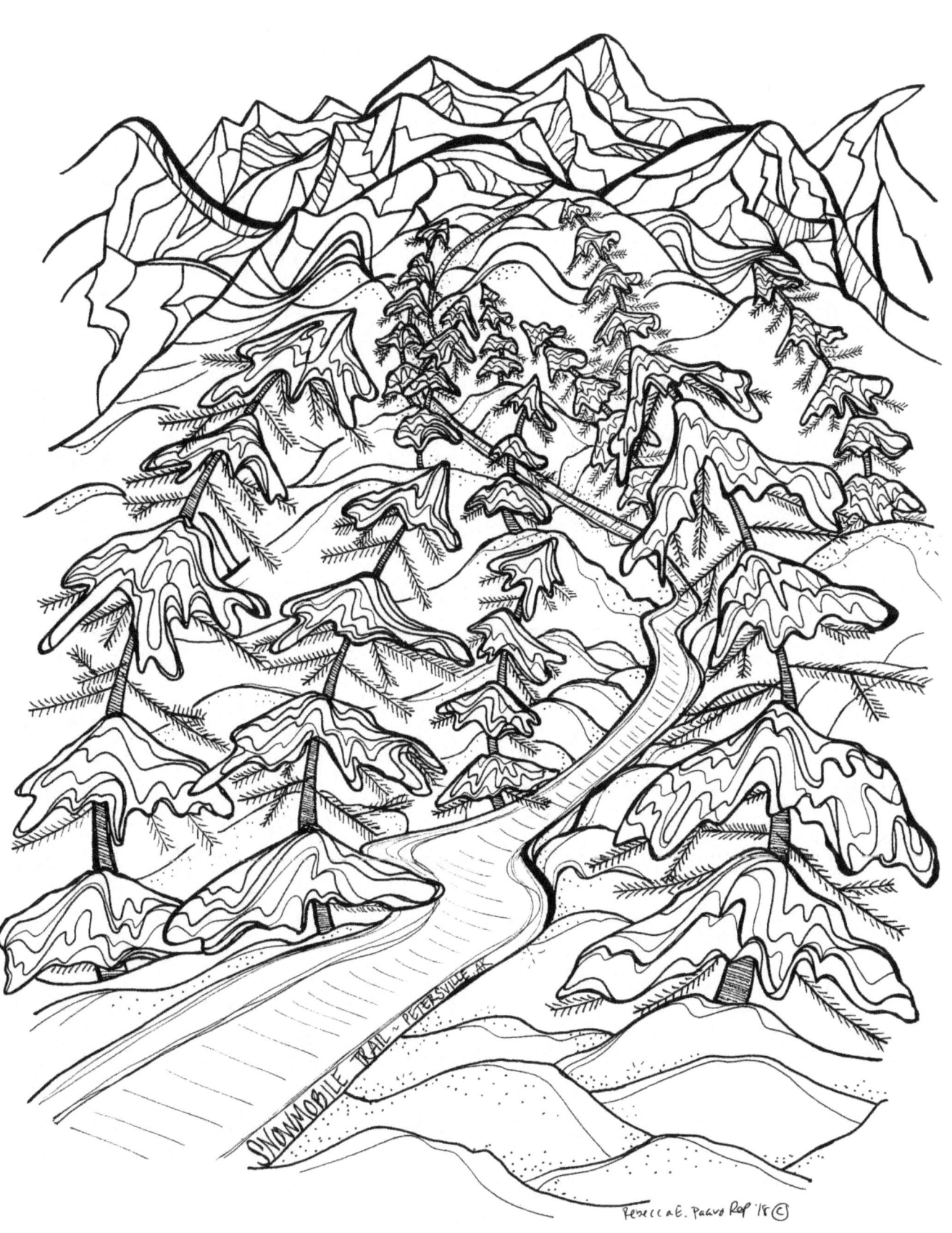

Rebecca Paavo© www.sorrelwoodstudio.com

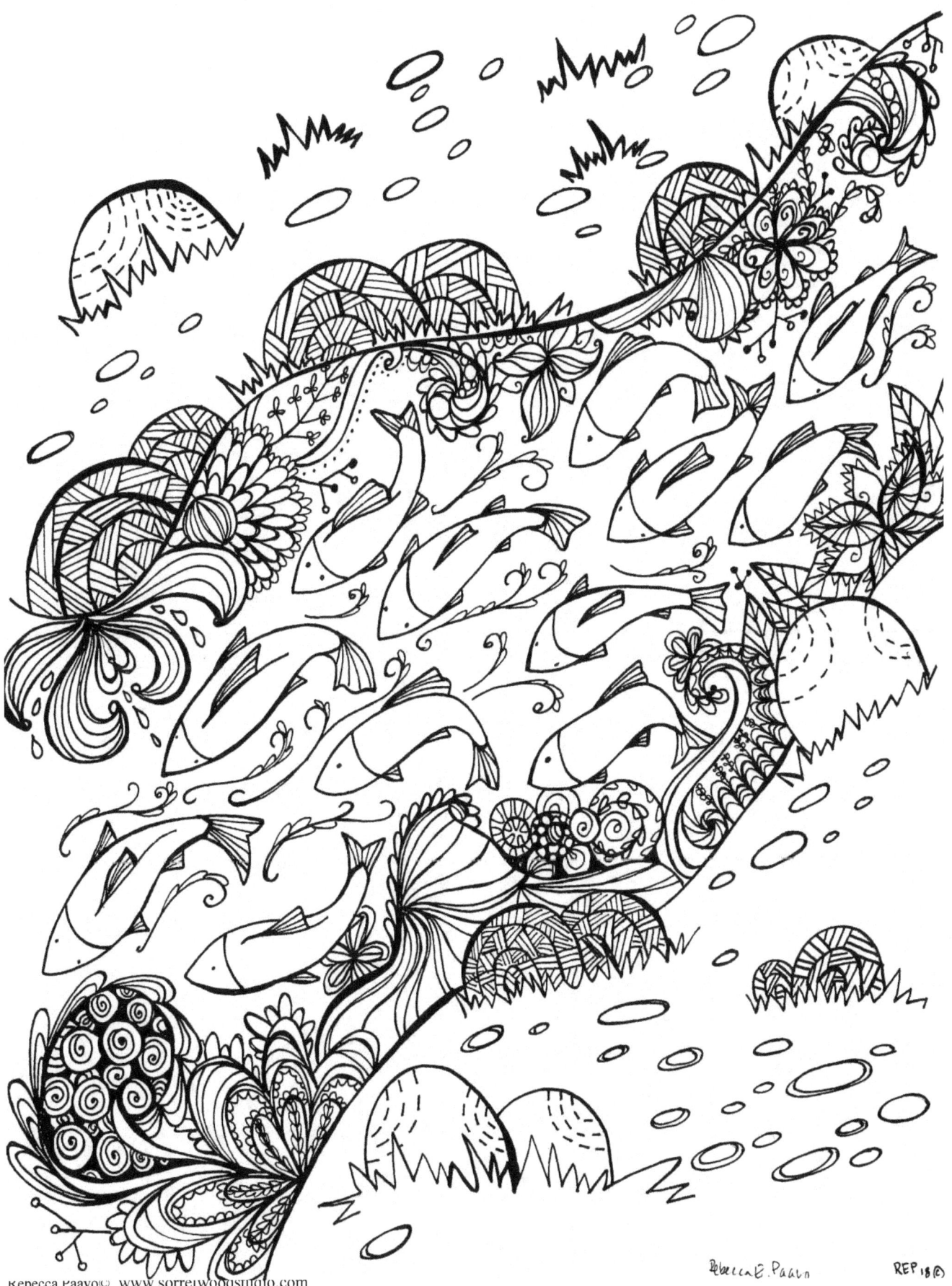

Rebecca Paavo© www.sorrelwoodstudio.com

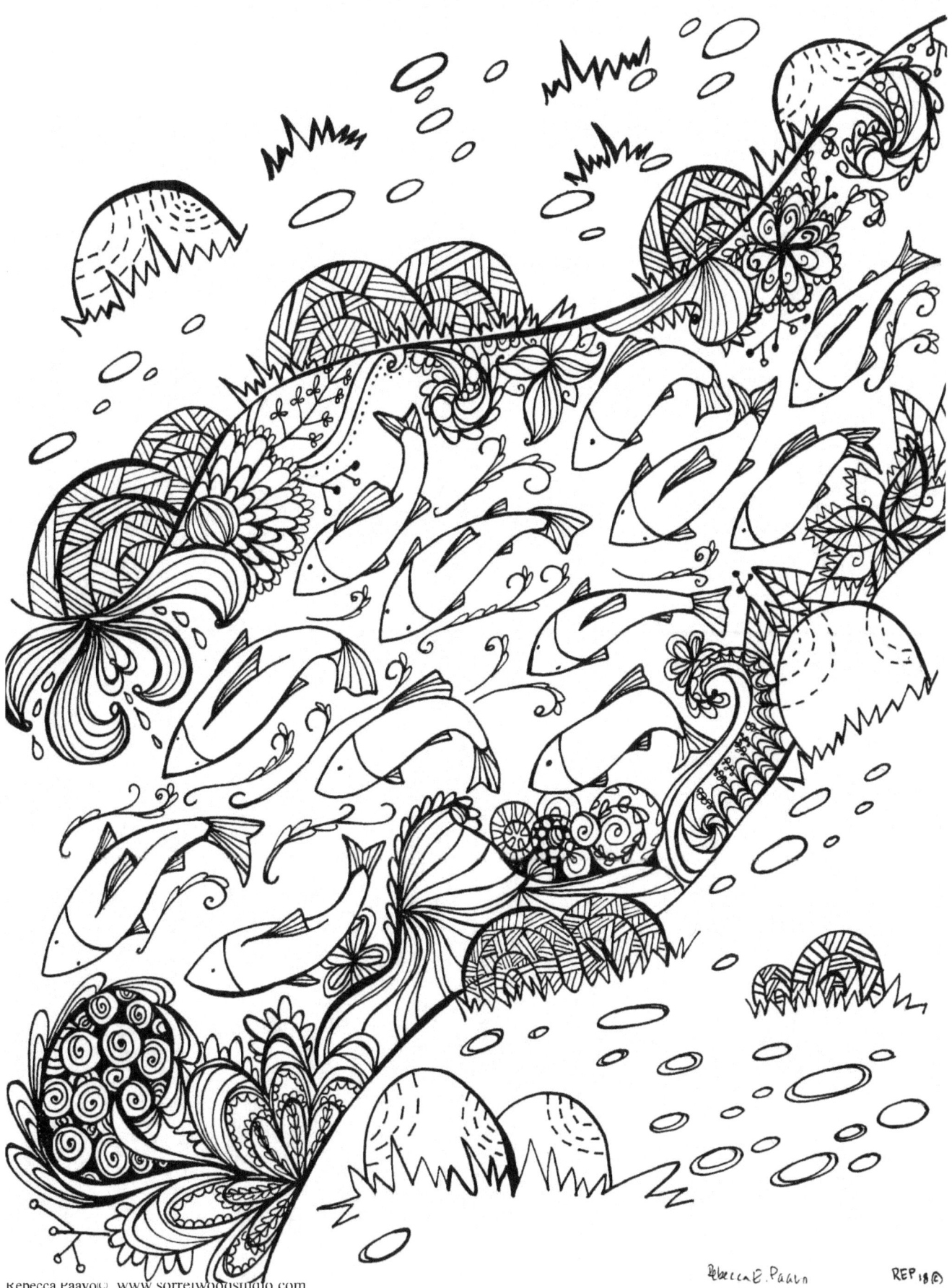

Rebecca Paavo© www.sorrelwoodstudio.com

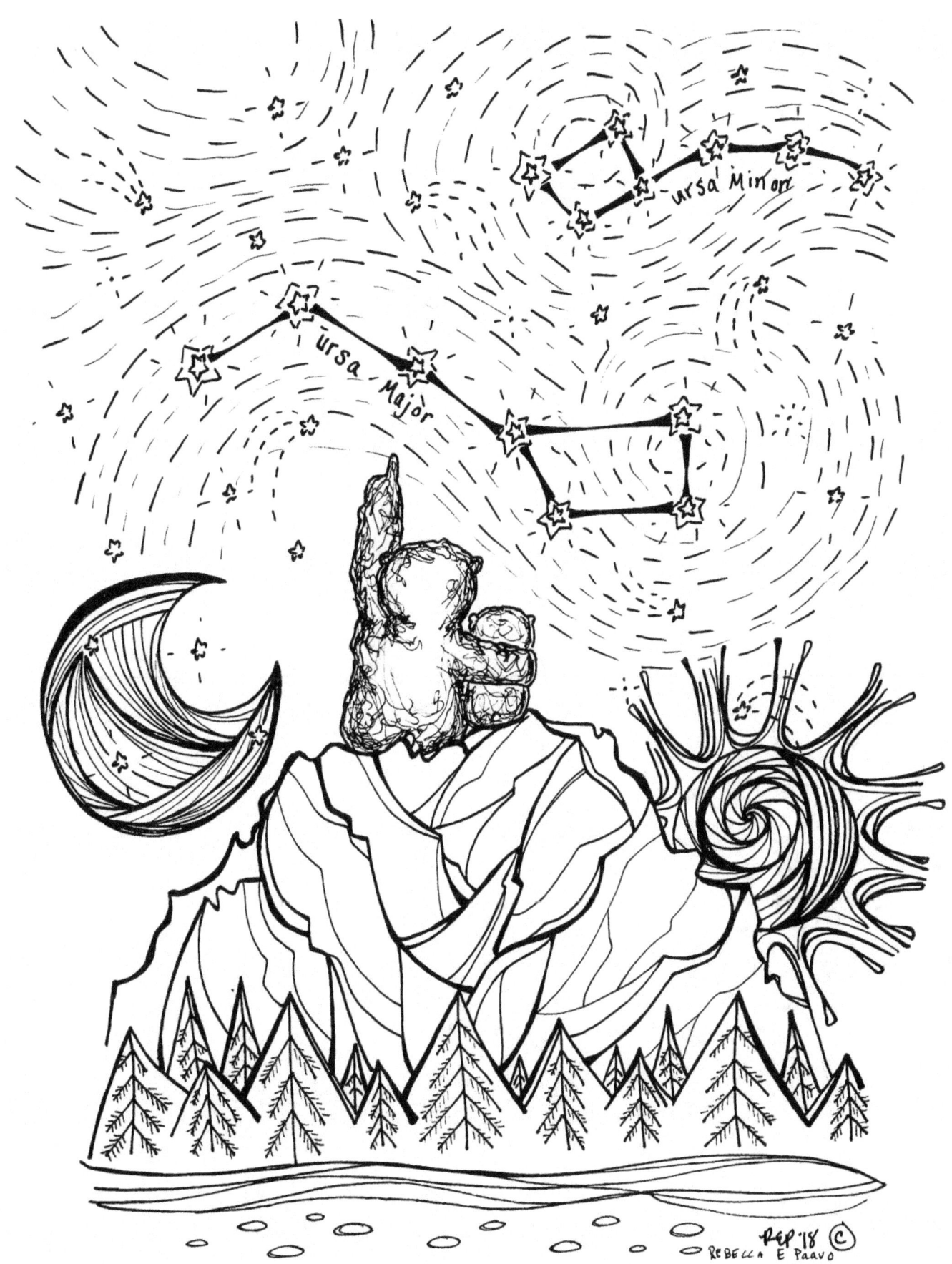

Rebecca Paavo© www.sorrelwoodstudio.com

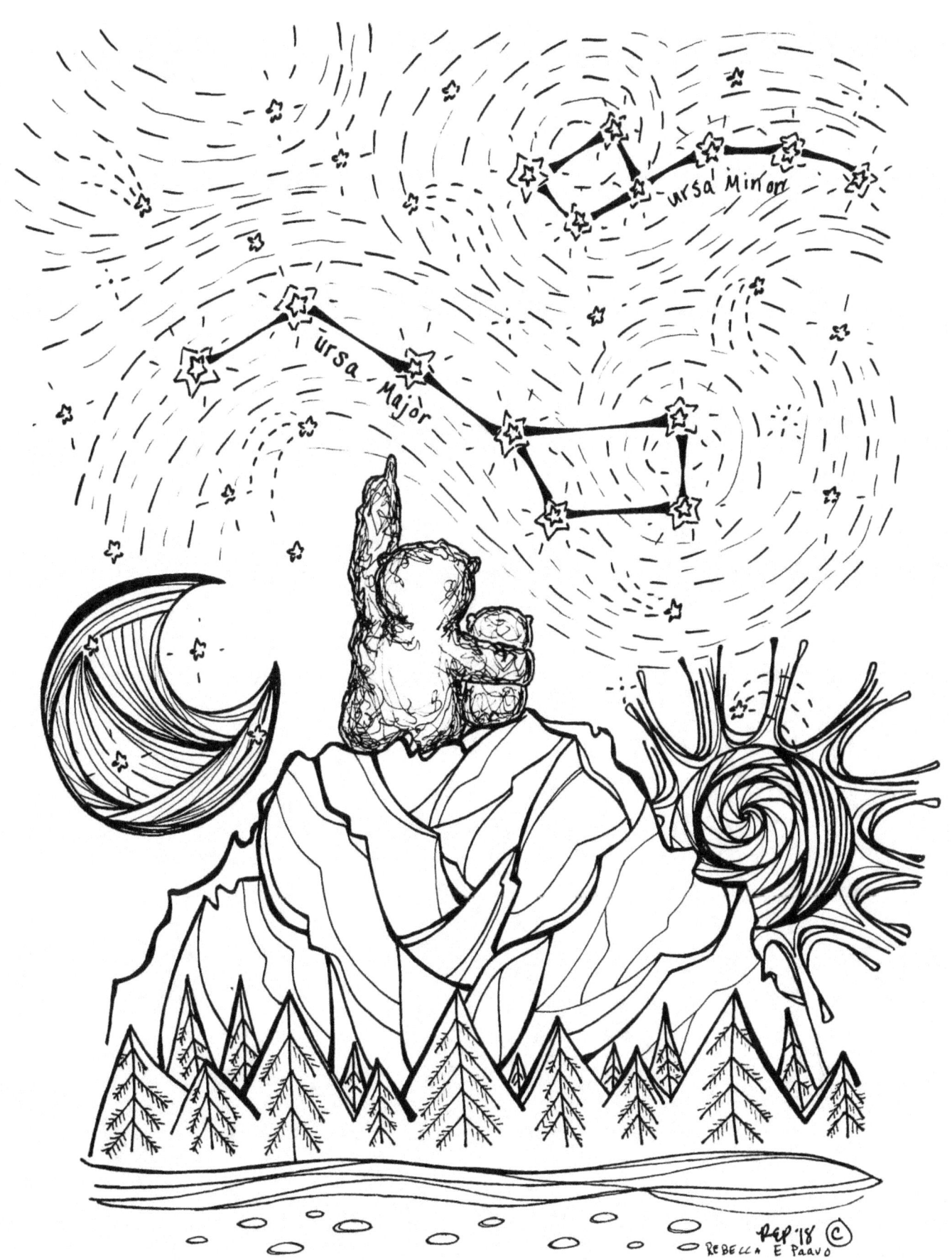

Rebecca Paavo© www.sorrelwoodstudio.com

A TANGLE OF ALASKA KNOWLEDGE

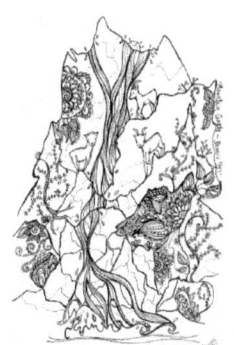

Image 1: Mountain Goats on the Seward Highway. The Seward Hwy is Alaska's most popular scenic drive. This 125 mile road connects South Central Alaska (Anchorage, the Matanuska - Susitna Valley, and the main body of Alaska) to the Kenai Peninsula. It takes you around the Turnagain Arm which is a waterway fed by the Cook Inlet. The road leaving Anchorage is bordered on one side by the Chugach Mountains and water on the other. Often mountain goats will climb the cliffs down to the road side and watch the cars from the safety of the rocks while drinking from one of the many waterfalls.

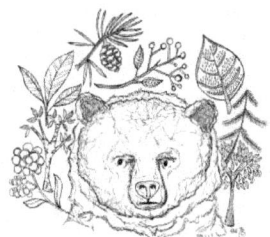

Image 2: Grizzly Bear Nearly 98% of the US brown bear population is contained in Alaska with an estimate of nearly 30,000 bears. The brown bear is the top predator in Alaska. Brown bears and Grizzly bears are in the same species class even though there are noticeable differences between them. Grizzly bears live mostly on the Alaska mainland while their larger cousins, the coastal brown bears and Kodiak brown bears, live along coast lines and the Kodiak Archipelago.

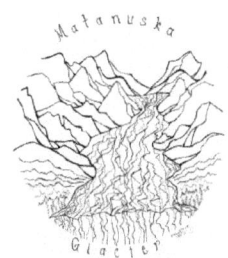

Image 3: Matanuska Glacier The Matanuska Glacier is located in Glacier View, Alaska about 100 miles from Anchorage, Alaska's largest city. It is a valley glacier, meaning that it fills the valley space between the mountains. The Matanuska glacier is the largest glacier that is accessible by car in the US. It spans 4 miles wide and is 27 miles long. Glaciers are essentially a river of ice and are always moving, and this giant flows at about one foot every day and is the life source of the mighty Matanuska River.

Rebecca Paavo© www.sorrelwoodstudio.com

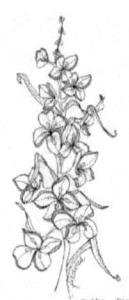

Image 4: Fireweed Fireweed is one of Alaska's trademark flowers of summer. The blossoms are a brilliant shade of pink and have many blooms per stock. The individual stocks can grow as tall as an average person, though most peak at around 4 feet high. Arctic fireweed is a smaller version that only grows a few inches tall and has fewer blossoms. Fireweed gets its name from the fact that it is the first vegetation to return to areas that have been burned by wildfire. Every part of the plant is edible. Tea and jelly made from the blossoms are a favorite among local wild crafters.

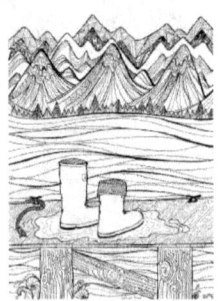

Image 5: Boots Xtra Tuff boots are a staple among local Alaskans. Dry feet means happy campers, or fishermen, or hunters, or ATV riders, or gardeners, you get the idea. ;)

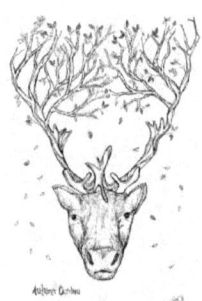

Image 6: Autumn Caribou Caribou are the wild undomesticated version of reindeer. They grow larger and are hardier than farm raised reindeer. Both male (bull) and female (cow) have antlers but the bull's antlers grow much larger. All caribou shed their antlers in the fall. There are 32 wild herds of caribou spread over Alaska, and together their numbers total around 950,000!

Rebecca Paavo© www.sorrelwoodstudio.com

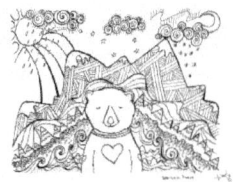

Image 7: Black bear Black bears are the smallest bear species in North America and also the most abundant. Alaska is home to approximately 100,000 black bears. Because of their small size they are often thought of as not as dangerous as their brown cousins, but these bears can be just as dangerous and protective of their young cubs. But they sure can be cute to see, from a very safe distance ;)

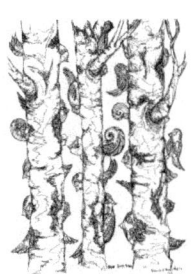

Image 8: Paper Birch Trees These beautiful white barked trees grow abundantly in Alaska. They can reach as high as 60ft tall! They lose their bright leaves in the fall but not before they turn from gorgeous green to glowing yellow, to fire orange, to crimson red, and finally brown. In the autumn they seem to set the mountain sides and forests aflame in their brilliance. The flaky bark can peel easily away like paper, hence the name Paper Birch.

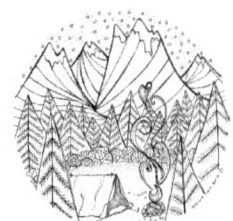

Image 9: Campout Pop a tent beneath the mountain peaks in a spruce forest and watch the shooting stars and search for the Big Dipper.

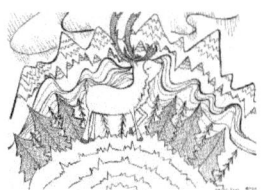

Image 10: Caribou & the Northern Lights If you're lucky enough to spot a caribou in the later part of fall before they shed their antlers, you might be lucky enough to see the northern lights dance across the sky as well. After living in the 'Land of the Midnight Sun' through the endless days of summer, autumn brings with it the return of the night sky. On many dark nights, from fall to spring, the aurora borealis put on a beautiful light display.

Rebecca Paavo© www.sorrelwoodstudio.com

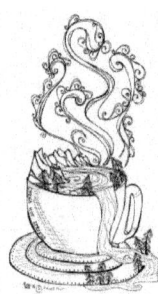

Image 11: Chena Hot Springs Chena Hot Springs is located about 60 miles north of Fairbanks and about 150 miles south of the Arctic Circle. The springs were discovered in 1905 by gold prospectors in the area, but there is evidence that indigenous Alaskans were using them for many years before their recorded history. By 1912 the hot spring had already become a resort for frozen locals seeking the relaxing baths in the ancient mineral spring fed lake that averages 105* F.

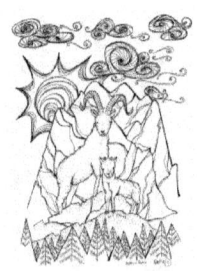

Image 12: Dall Sheep Dall Sheep live in all Alaska mountain ranges. The rams (males) have massive curled horns and the ewes (females) have shorter horns that only curve slightly. Rams look more like ewes until around three years of age when their horns begin to grow continuously and they become more recognizable. Unlike caribou and moose, sheep do not shed their horns in the fall; they grow steadily from spring through early fall, stopping growth in the winter, and restarting in the summer. Each stop and start season leaves a ringed pattern on the horns which you can count to tell how old the animal is, just like a counting tree rings.

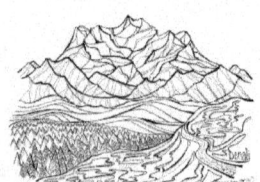

Image 13: Denali Denali is a native Athabascan word meaning "great one" or "tall one". Being the highest mountain on the North American continent with a summit elevation of 20,310 feet above sea level it is easy to see why the native locals gave this magnificent mountain its name. Denali is also the tallest land-based mountain on Earth with a vertical rise of 18,000 feet. The difference between measuring "high" and "tall" comes from how a mountain is measured. Denali is the third "highest" mountain in the world which is determined by measuring a mountain's highest point above sea level. It is the "tallest" mountain on Earth by measuring the distance from the base to the summit. The upper half of Denali is always covered in snow and has many glaciers. Temperatures can reach -75*F and wind chills of -118*F.

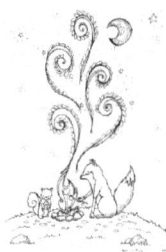

Image 14: Fox Alaska is home to the red fox and the arctic fox. The arctic fox has extra fur around its paws in the winter to protect it from snow and ice. Being the smaller of the two kinds they grow to only 6-10 pounds. The arctic fox sheds its white thick winter coat in spring and has a short brown coat for the summer. Then they shed their lighter summer coat in the fall for their luxurious white winter coat again. The arctic fox lives above the Arctic Circle and on mainland coastal regions. The red fox can grow to 16 pounds and is found throughout Alaska.

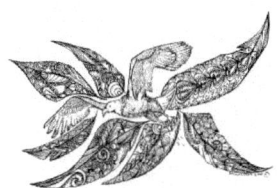

Image 15: The bald eagle is the national bird of the US and is only found in North America, with the highest abundancy found in Alaska with an estimated population of 30,000 birds. The bald eagle can grow to have a wingspan of up to 7.5 feet and weigh up to 14 pounds. They build enormous nests up to 8 feet across and weighing as much as a ton!

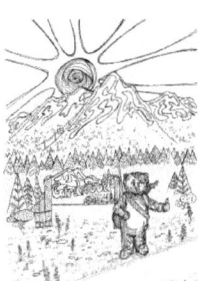

Image 16: Girdwood Girdwood, Alaska is a small ski resort town in the Chugach Mountains about 40 miles south of Anchorage along the beautiful Seward Highway. The Fungus Fair, Blueberry Festival, Forest Fair and other summer festivities keep this little town busy with tourists in both winter and summer. There is a tram to the top of the ski slope which is open year round and the view of the Turnagain Arm and surrounding peaks is amazing from the mountain top.

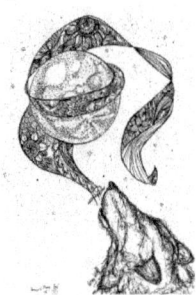

Image 17: Gray Wolf Wolves live throughout the state of Alaska with an estimate of 7,000-11,000 in population. Wolves live in packs of between 6 and 30 wolves. Male wolves can range from 85-145 pounds, and females can grow to be 110 pounds.

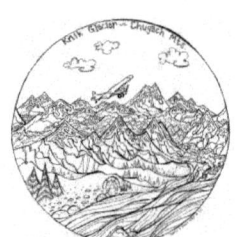

Image 18: Knik Glacier The Knik glacier is 50 miles north of Anchorage, flowing out of the northern end of the Chugach Mountains. It is one of the largest glaciers in Alaska with an ice field more than 25 miles long and 5 miles across. Its 400 foot ice walls calve daily, crashing into an iceberg filled lake which flows into the 25 mile long Knik River which then empties into the Cook Inlet. The glacier is not accessible by car, but locals have long enjoyed the hour's long, difficult, ATV trek to the lake of this magnificent ice giant. The ice field can be reached by small aircraft that locals refer to as bush planes: tiny planes that can bring you to the middle of nowhere AKA, 'the bush.'

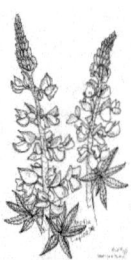

Image 19: Arctic Lupine Another telltale time of summer in Alaska is artic lupine. The soft to brilliant purple hued blossomed stems grow along side road ways and in open fields. Unlike Fireweed this gorgeous plant is not edible and is poisonous.

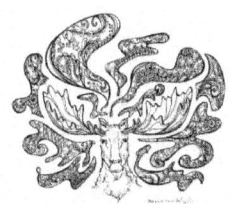

Image 20: Moose Moose can be found in nearly all regions of Alaska. The largest member of the deer family, full grown moose can range in size from 800 – 1,600 pounds. Newborns can weigh only 28 pounds at birth and can grow as much as 10x their birthweight in as little as five months! It is not uncommon to see twins born, but it is more common to see single births. Bull (male) moose have antlers and cows (female) do not. The Bull Moose can grow an 80 pound rack (antlers) in one summer, adding an inch a day. They shed their antlers every fall.

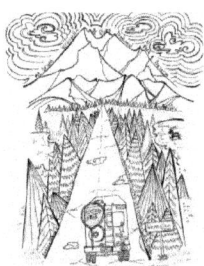

Page 21: Mt. Drum   Mt. Drum is located in the Wrangell mountain range of the Wrangell-St. Elias National Park and Preserve in Alaska's Copper River Basin. It is a stratovolcano and has an elevation of 12,011 feet. On the long drive east on the Glenn Highway you get unobstructed views of this dormant giant.

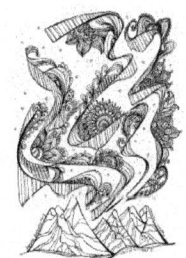

Page 22: Northern Lights   Green, purple, red, and blue bands of light, the aurora borealis are some of the most amazing natural phenomena to experience. Visible in late fall, winter, and early spring these brilliant lights move and wave across the heavens on clear nights. They are best viewed in the darkness of winter because in summer most areas of Alaska have 20+ hours of daylight and it doesn't get dark enough to see them. The lights are actually solar particles blown into the Earth's magnetic field.

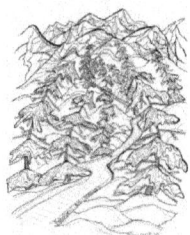

Page 23: Snowmobile Trail, Petersville In Alaska we call snowmobiles 'snowmachines'. Petersville is an area south of Denali that is a popular place for snowmachiners to spend their time riding countless miles of trails and enjoying the views of the Alaska Range and Denali.

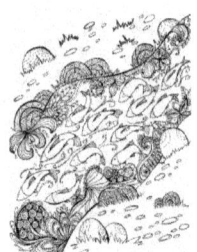

Page 24: Salmon Run Alaska has five species of salmon: sockeye (aka red), coho (aka silver), king (aka chinook), chum, and pink. Salmon eggs are laid in fresh water lakes or rivers. When they hatch, the salmon will remain in the freshwater for varying times depending on their species before migrating to the sea. They migrate through river systems to the ocean and remain there for a given amount of time depending upon their species, after which they make the return migration to spawn in the lake or river they were born in. The return of the salmon happens in large groups, sometimes hundreds of thousands, called 'runs' that last several weeks during the summer.

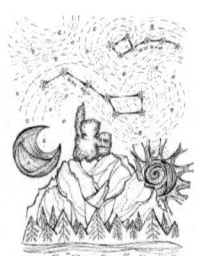

Page 25: Big Dipper & Little Dipper Earth's daily rotation gives us the illusion that the Big Dipper and Little Dipper rotate around the North Star, Polaris, making a complete circle each day. Because of Alaska's location in the extreme north of the northern hemisphere these constellations are visible from most every area of the state on any clear night and it is possible to watch them rotate position in the sky over the course of the night without ever losing sight. The Big Dipper is also known as Ursa Major, meaning Big Bear, and the Little Dipper is also known as Ursa Minor, meaning Little Bear.

Information sources include:
Alaska Department of Fish and Game, adfg.alaska.gov
Alaska Department of Natural Resources, dnr.alaska.gov
Alaska.org

Rebecca Paavo© www.sorrelwoodstudio.com

About the Artist

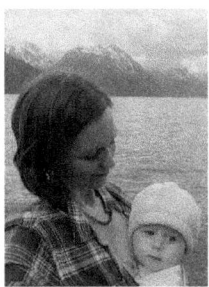

Rebecca is a beach born and raised Floridian who migrated to the last frontier of Alaska in 2010.

She is a wife to one handsome man in camouflage, and a mother to three princesses who climb trees. She is an artist, a homeschool mom, and an Air Force veteran; a yoga loving, tea drinking, gardener, reader, camper, and hiker.

She spends her spare time drawing, painting, writing, and doodling on paper, canvas, walls, and wood.

Tangled Up in Alaska is Rebecca's first coloring book but she hopes to publish several others.

You can follow Rebecca's artwork pursuits on Facebook at Sorrelwood Studio or her website at www.sorrelwoodstudio.com

Your Amazon reviews and sample pictures are always welcome and appreciated.

Rebecca Paavo© www.sorrelwoodstudio.com

www.ingramcontent.com/pod-product-compliance
Lightning Source LLC
Chambersburg PA
CBHW062110220526
45471CB00010B/3678